SELECTED ESSAYS

SELECTED ESSAYS

EDITED BY

CLAUDE M. FUESS

Essay Index Reprint Series

BOOKS FOR LIBRARIES PRESS
FREEPORT, NEW YORK

Acknowledgment for the use of copyright material is
hereby made to Messrs. Charles Scribner's Sons for Stevenson's *Crabbed Age and Youth*; to Mr. A. C. Benson
and Messrs. G. P. Putnam's Sons for Mr. Benson's *Books;*
to Dr. Samuel McChord Crothers for his *Evolution of the
Gentleman;* to Miss Agnes Repplier for her *Mission of
Humour;* and to Dean LeBaron Russell Briggs for his *The
Transition from School to College.*

INTERNATIONAL STANDARD BOOK NUMBER:
0-8369-2394-4

LIBRARY OF CONGRESS CATALOG CARD NUMBER:
72-134078

PRINTED IN THE UNITED STATES OF AMERICA
BY
NEW WORLD BOOK MANUFACTURING CO., INC.
HALLANDALE, FLORIDA 33009

PREFATORY NOTE

THE new list of English books which may be offered in preparation for entrance examination to college wisely recognizes the prevailing tendency towards studying literature largely by types, such as the Short Story, the Letter, or the Narrative Poem. This present volume in response is planned to meet the requirement for "a collection of Essays by Bacon, Lamb, De Quincey, Hazlitt, Emerson, and later writers." The essays here reprinted are therefore of two classes: one including selections from the five authors named specifically by the College Entrance Board; the other illustrating the Essay in its later development, with especial emphasis on contemporary essays and essayists. A characteristic essay by Montaigne, the originator of the form, is prefixed by way of introduction.

In secondary schools the study of a literary type like the Essay does not need to be comprehensive or detailed. The chief objects to be attained by the teacher should be to arouse interest in the subject, to call attention to the great masters and interpret their work, and to bring out clearly the significant facts regarding the nature and history of the Essay as a variety of prose literature. The annotation in this volume is brief and compact, intended merely to throw light on difficult passages. The selections are, it is hoped, of a representative character; but they ought to be supplemented by further reading, particularly in current magazines, so that students may be able intelligently to compare modern essays with those by acknowledged classic writers. In any case the Essay should be viewed as closely related to life itself, and especially to life as we see it immediately around us in our own time.

CONTENTS

vi   CONTENTS

INTRODUCTION

MOST people are able to recognize an essay when they see one; but although the thing itself is not usually difficult to detect, it is by no means easy to define and analyze. We ordinarily take it for granted that the Essay is a form of exposition, or, more specifically, a short discussion in prose on some selected topic. Aiming as it does to treat a subject, not exhaustively, but on a limited scale, its length is largely determined by the average reader's power of attention for a single sitting. It must, moreover, be complete in itself, not a section or a chapter of a larger work. The word, derived from the Latin *exagium*, a weighing, was given its modern significance by Montaigne, who used it as meaning an experiment, or rather a tentative consideration of a problem. The object of the Essay, as Mr. Morley interprets it, is "merely to open questions, to indicate points, to suggest cases, to sketch outlines.",

With these broad and general specifications no one is likely to quarrel. Unfortunately, however, the word "essay" as it is too often employed to-day is so exceedingly comprehensive that it is applied indiscriminately to brief expositions or arguments of any kind. Its use ought certainly to be limited with more care. Our current magazines, for instance, are enlivened with short treatises on such diverse matters as the Panama Canal, the importance of vivisection, and the evils of monopoly. Written mainly to furnish information to the public, these discussions are objective, unimaginative, and impersonal. They are, furthermore, frankly ephemeral in their purpose, and make no pretense of being permanent literature. Such treatises, which are better classified as "articles," plainly do not belong in the same category with the genuine Essay.

The true Essay, on the other hand, has a distinct literary aim. Its object is not primarily to spread knowledge, but to delight and stimulate its readers. Its tone and temper may vary widely, and its subject-matter may cover nearly every field; but behind it is always some individual point of view. Some standard divisions of the Essay will at once occur to everybody: the Didactic or Philosophical Essay, represented by selections from Bacon and Emerson; the Biographical or Historical Essay, like Macaulay's *Warren Hastings;* the Critical Essay, illustrated by Matthew Arnold's *Byron;* and finally the Familiar Essay, which is, strictly speaking, the Essay in its ripest, truest sense. All these types, different though they are in manner, style, and material, have one end in common: the expression of a personal theory or attitude towards life.

It is with the Familiar Essay that this collection is chiefly concerned, for it is when bestowed on this branch of literature that the term "essay" is most accurately used. Like the Familiar Letter, to which it is closely related, it is essentially "a direct exposure of the man behind the book." In this narrower meaning the Essay is subjective, personal, and discursive, full of casual gossip and intimate self-revelation. The best examples of it, such as

Hazlitt's *On Going a Journey* or Stevenson's *Crabbed Age and Youth*, have decided individual touches, a direct personal appeal, and an attractive informality as of fireside talk. They resemble passages in a friendly correspondence, except that they are, as a rule, more orderly, more coherent, and more confined to a single theme.

To the Familiar Essayist, however, the assigned title is not always of supreme importance. Montaigne discourses on cannibals, Hazlitt upon sundials, and Stevenson upon gas-lamps; yet each persists in talking mainly of himself, and each deals with his subject egotistically in terms of his own unique individuality. The Essay thus often tends to become a form or phase of autobiography. This assertion will not, of course, apply without modification to works like Macaulay's *Addison* or Emerson's *History*, which, as we have seen, stand in a group by themselves; but even these essays will be found upon examination to be developments of the favorite theories of their writers, and therefore to a large extent personal in nature.

The tone of the Essay is obviously capable of wide variations, depending upon the character and mood of the author. It may be profoundly serious, as in Emerson's *Compensation;* pleasantly witty, as in Miss Repplier's *Mission of Humour;* or elaborately rhetorical, as in De Quincey's *Vision of Sudden Death*. Emerson and Bacon discuss love in mystical fashion; Stevenson plays with it in a manner satirical and facetious. In practically every case, however, the Essay has an aristocratic flavor. Essayists, like writers of *vers de société*, seem to be tranquil, cultivated persons, disinclined to be passionate, impetuous, or openly enthusiastic. The Essay does not burst spontaneously from the hearts of simple men; it is rather an artificial product, possible only in an educated, perhaps even a sophisticated community.

The Familiar Essayists, usually people of scholarly tastes and seasoned wisdom, have been fond of allusion and illustration. They have loved to point an argument with an anecdote, and to press home a doctrine with a simile. But the knowledge displayed is never obtrusive or pedantic, for the Essay must always seem "the brief and light result of learning and meditation." It is beyond the essayist's province to usurp the preacher's office or to play the part of tutor. He is quite content with a hint instead of a sermon, with a jest in place of a solemn maxim. He is well aware also that the slightest trace of conventionality or affectation or even of reticence will destroy the impression he wishes to produce.

This means, of course, that he is to be on intimate and natural terms with his audience. Assuming the confidential tone of unreserved conversation, the skillful essayist behaves to his readers as if he were betraying to them momentous secrets. Montaigne, Lamb, Stevenson seem almost to be chatting at our very elbows, so frankly and innocently do they disclose their partialities and foibles, their little whims and weaknesses.

"An essayist without style is a contradiction in terms," asserts a shrewd critic. The names of the great English essayists as we run them over — Bacon, Addison, Lamb, Hazlitt, Arnold, Pater, Stevenson, Benson — are those of men who are masters of excellent and distinctive prose. With these authors the manner of expression is of immense importance. Their sentences as they run smoothly and lucidly along may seem to be artless and unstudied; but the ease and grace so fascinating to the reader have been attained at the expense of untiring labor and rigorous discipline. So also with the structure of the Essay; the writer may apparently be wandering with the vagaries of his own impulsive will, but beneath there is an informing purpose directing and restraining the flow of thought.

The Essay, as Mr. Gosse points out, was invented in March, 1571, in the second story of the tower of the old castle of Montaigne, when that French gentleman, weary of statecraft, settled down at his leisure to compose his inimitable *Essais*. Seeking deliberately for a means of self-revelation, he discovered this entirely new way of writing casually on the most diverse matters, treating them always, however, with his own prejudices, eccentricities, and hobbies visible in the background. Almost unwittingly he originated a distinct type of literature which has exerted a mighty influence on the authors and readers of succeeding centuries.

The earliest man to employ the form in England was undoubtedly Francis Bacon, who, in 1598, five years after Montaigne's death, published **ten** essays. In appropriating Montaigne's title, Bacon was unable to assimilate more than the superficial features of the Frenchman's spirit. Fortunately he was able in turn to make the Essay express admirably his own cold and logical turn of mind; thus, where Montaigne had instinctively been leisurely and desultory, Bacon was abrupt, incisive, and sententious.

Neither Montaigne nor Bacon, strangely enough, had any marked effect on the next generation or two in England. The poet Cowley and the statesman Sir William Temple produced essays, but neither was read extensively. Not until the advent of Joseph Addison (1672–1719) and Richard Steele (1672–1729), and their collaboration in the *Tatler* (1709–10) and the *Spectator* (1711–12), did the Essay become widely popular. By instituting the tri-weekly and daily periodical and devoting it principally to the Essay, they gave that literary form real dignity. The extraordinary success of their venture induced dozens of journalists through the eighteenth century to busy themselves in editing similar publications, and thus thousands of essays appeared, all but a few of which have justly been forgotten. Occasionally such men as Dr. Johnson and Goldsmith rose above the common level of mediocrity; but on the whole the essays of that period were dull and uninspired, burdened with didacticism and devoid of wit.

The golden age of the Essay in England began in the first quarter of the nineteenth century with the work of Lamb and Hazlitt, the two most brilliant masters of their school. With them the Essay became what it was to Montaigne, a picturesque medium for the disclosure of their own personalities. They gave it the impress of grace and beauty by embedding their ideas in a nearly perfect intimate style. At the same time the rise of the great British Reviews — the *Edinburgh* (1802), the *Quarterly* (1809), and *Blackwood's* (1817) — was a powerful stimulus to another variety of essay-writing, and led to the appearance of Macaulay and Carlyle, who represent the Critical and Biographical Essay at its best.

De Quincey wrote literally dozens of essays of a miscellaneous character, and managed to turn the form to the uses of a kind of "higher journalism." Meanwhile Irving, in America, was reviving the Essay of Addison and Goldsmith, and Emerson was experimenting with the "Wisdom Essay," and packing, like Bacon, a shrewd philosophy into the space of a few short pages.

Of the later essayists only a few need special mention. Matthew Arnold devoted himself largely to critical work, but he managed to bring that particular type of essay almost to perfection. The tradition of Montaigne, Lamb, and Hazlitt was continued by Robert Louis Stevenson, who, in both charm of style and grace of manner, proved himself not unworthy to be their literary successor.

To-day we seem to be watching a wholesome revival of the Essay. Miss Repplier writing on *The Passing of the Essay* and Mr. Middleton discussing *The Decay of the Essay* prove in their own work the very falsity of the contention which they are trying to establish. It is, of course, true that now as always the Familiar Essay is not popular with the great body of the reading public. Its appeal is rather to cultured, discriminating people, who constitute a small but influential part of the entire population. Nevertheless there is no occasion for pessimism. Mr. Arthur Christopher Benson, Mr. Augustine Birrell, Mr. Chesterton, Mr. Austin Dobson, Mr. Crothers, Mr. Gerald Stanley Lee, Mr. Richard Middleton, Mr. Richard Burton, Miss Repplier, and others have won their audiences and are likely to retain them. We may be sure that some Familiar Essays published during the last ten years

Conclusion

will compare not unfavorably with those of earlier periods.

As for the Essay in its broader sense, it has become practically indispensable as a medium for the interchange of opinion. It is a vehicle for ideas: the scholar may, in brief compass, announce the results of his researches; the statesman may outline his policies; the reformer may propose remedies for crying evils — all this with much less labor than would be involved in writing a longer book. We have several magazines devoted entirely to articles and essays; and there are few periodicals of the better sort which do not include at least one essay in every issue. Of all this vast amount of material produced annually, the greater part is necessarily of transient interest, lacking in style or in some essential which might have made it enduring. A small number of essays, however, will last beyond the month of publication; and these are almost invariably essays of the familiar sort, dealing, not with temporary or current events, but with the larger questions of life which loom up in every age. The work which does live is sufficient to show that the Essay as a type of literature is still well worth study, and that its glorious day is by no means over.

SELECTED ESSAYS

MICHEL DE MONTAIGNE

AGAINST IDLENESS

THE Emperor Vespasian,[1] being sick of the disease whereof he died, did not for all that neglect to enquire after the state of the empire; and even in bed continually despatched very many affairs of great consequence; for which, being reproved by his physician, as a thing prejudicial to his health, "An emperor," said he, "must die standing." A fine saying, in my opinion, and worthy a great prince. The Emperor Adrian[2] since made use of the same words, and kings should be often put in mind of them, to make them know that the great office conferred upon them of the command of so many men, is not an employment of ease; and that there is nothing can so justly disgust a subject, and make him unwilling to expose himself to labour and danger for the service of his prince, than to see him, in the mean time, devoted to his ease and frivolous amusement: and to be solicitous of his preservation who so much neglects that of his people.

Whoever will take upon him to maintain that 't is better for a prince to carry on his wars by others, than in his own person, fortune will furnish him with examples enough of those whose lieutenants have brought great enterprises to a happy issue, and of those also whose presence has done more hurt than good: but no virtuous and valiant prince can with patience endure so dishonourable councils. Under colour of saving his head, like the statute of a saint, for the happiness of his kingdom, they degrade him from and declare him incapable of his office, which is military throughout. I know one [3] who had rather be beaten, than to sleep while another fights for him; and who never without jealousy heard of any brave thing done even by his own officers in his absence. And Soliman I [4] said, with very good reason, in my opinion, that victories obtained without the master were never complete. Much more would he have said that that master ought to blush for shame to pretend to any share in the honour, having contributed nothing to the work, but his voice and thought; nor even so much of those, considering that in such work as that the direction and command that deserve honour are only such as are given upon the spot, and in the heat of the business. No pilot performs his office by standing still. The princes of the Ottoman family,[5] the chiefest in the world in military fortune, have warmly embraced this opinion, and Bajazet II, with his son who swerved from it, spending their time in science and other retired employments, gave great blows to their empire; and Amurath III, now reigning, following their example, begins to find the same. Was it not Edward III [6] king of England, who said this of our Charles V: [7] "There never was a king who so seldom put on his armour, and yet never king who cut me out so much work." He had reason to think it strange, as an effect of chance more than of reason. And let those seek out some other to join with them than me, who will reckon the kings of Castile and Portugal among the warlike and magnanimous conquerors, because at the distance of twelve hundred leagues from their lazy abode by the conduct of their captains they made themselves masters of both the Indies; of which it has to be known if they would have had even the courage to go and in person enjoy them.

The Emperor Julian [8] said yet further, that a philosopher and a brave man ought not so much as to breathe; that is to say, not to allow any more to bodily necessities than what we cannot refuse; keeping the soul and body still intent and busy about honourable, great, and virtuous things. He was ashamed if any one in public saw him spit, or sweat (which is said by some, also, of the Lacedæmonian young men, and which Xenephon [9] says of the Persian), forasmuch as he conceived that exercise, continual labour, and sobriety ought to have dried up all those superfluities. What Seneca [10] says will not be unfit for this place; which is, that the ancient Romans kept their youth always standing, and taught them nothing that they were to learn sitting.

'T is a generous desire to wish to die usefully and like a man, but the effect lies not so much in our resolution as in our good fortune; a thousand have proposed to themselves in battle, either to overcome or to die, who have failed both in the one and the other, wounds and imprisonment crossing their design and compelling them to live against their will. There are diseases that overthrow even our desires and our knowledge. Fortune ought not to second the vanity of the Roman legions, who bound them-

selves by oath either to overcome or die: — "I
will return, Marcus Fabius, a conqueror, from the
fight; and if I fail, I wish the indignation of Jove,
Mars, and the other offended gods may light upon
me." The Portuguese say that in a certain place of
their conquest of the Indies, they met with soldiers,
who had condemned themselves, with horrible exe-
crations, to enter into no other composition but either
to cause themselves to be slain, or to remain victorious; and had their heads and beards shaved in token
of this vow. 'T is to much purpose for us to hazard
ourselves and to be obstinate; it seems as if blows
avoided those who present themselves too briskly
to them, and do not willingly fall upon those who
too willingly seek them, and so defeat them of their
design. Such there have been, who, after having
tried all ways, not having been able with all their
endeavour to obtain the favour of dying by the
hand of the enemy, have been constrained, to make
good their resolution of bringing home the honour
of victory or of losing their lives, to kill themselves
even in the heat of battle. Of which there are other
examples, but this is one; Philistus, general of the
naval army of Dionysius the younger against the
Syracusans, presented them battle, which was
sharply disputed, their forces being equal; in this en-
gagement he had the better at the first, through his
own valour; but the Syracusans drawing about
his galley to environ him, after having done great
things in his own person to disengage himself and
hoping for no relief, with his own hand he took away
the life he had so liberally and in vain exposed to
the enemy.

Muley Moloch, king of Fez,[11] who lately won against

Sebastian, king of Portugal, the battle so famous for
the death of three kings, and for the transmission
of that great kingdom to the crown of Castile, was
extremely sick when the Portuguese entered in a
hostile manner into his dominions; and from that
day forward grew worse and worse, still drawing
nearer to and foreseeing his end: yet never did
man better employ his own sufficiency more vig-
orously and bravely than he did upon this occasion.
He found himself too weak to undergo the pomp
and ceremony of entering into his camp, which after
their manner is very magnificent, and therefore resigned that honour to his brother; but this was all
of the office of a general that he resigned; all the
rest of greatest utility and necessity he most exactly
and gloriously performed in his own person; his
body lying upon a couch, but his judgment and
courage upright and firm to his last gasp, and in
some sort beyond it. He might have wasted his
enemy, indiscreetly advanced into his dominions,
without striking a blow; and it was a very unhappy
occurrence, that for want of a little life or somebody
to substitute in the conduct of this war and the
affairs of a troubled state, he was compelled to seek
a doubtful and bloody victory, having another
by a better and surer way already in his hands.
Notwithstanding, he wonderfully managed the con-
tinuance of his sickness in consuming the enemy, and
in drawing them far from the assistance of their navy
and the ports they had on the coast of Africa, even
till the last day of his life, which he designedly reserved for this great battle. He arranged his battallia
in a circular form, environing the Portuguese army
on every side, which round circle coming to close in

and to draw up close together, not only hindered them in the conflict (which was very sharp through the valour of the young invading king) considering that they had every way to present a front, but prevented their flight after the defeat, so that, finding all passages possessed and shut up by the enemy, they were constrained to close up together again, "piled up not only in slaughter but in flight," and there they were slain in heaps upon one another, leaving to the conqueror a very bloody and entire victory. Dying, he caused himself to be carried and hurried from place to place where most need was, and passing along the files, encouraged the captains and soldiers one after another; but a corner of his main battallia being broken, he was not to be held from mounting on horseback with his sword in his hand; he did his utmost to break from those about him, and to rush into the thickest of the battle, they all the while withholding him, some by the bridle, some by his robe, and others by his stirrups. This last effort totally overwhelmed the little life he had left; they again laid him upon his bed; but coming to himself, and starting as it were out of his swoon, all other faculties failing, to give his people notice that they were to conceal his death (the most necessary command he had then to give, that his soldiers might not be discouraged with the news), he expired with his finger upon his mouth, the ordinary sign of keeping silence. Who ever lived so long and so far into death? who ever died so erect, or more like a man?

The most extreme degree of courageously treating death, and the most natural, is to look upon it not only without astonishment but without care, con-

tinuing the wonted course of life even into it, as
Cato [12] did, who entertained himself in study, and
went to sleep, having a violent and bloody death
in his heart, and the weapon in his hand with which he
was resolved to despatch himself.

FRANCIS BACON

OF TRAVEL

TRAVEL, in the younger sort, is a part of education,
in the elder, a part of experience. He that travelleth
into a country before he hath some entrance into the
language, goeth to school, and not to travel. That
young men travel under some tutor, or grave servant,
I allow [1] well; so that he be such a one that hath the
language, and hath been in the country before;
whereby he may be able to tell them what things are
worthy to be seen in the country where they go;
what acquaintances they are to seek; what exercises or discipline the place yieldeth. For else
young men should go hooded, and look abroad little.
It is a strange thing, that in sea voyages, where there
is nothing to be seen but sky and sea, men should
make diaries; but in land-travel, wherein so much
is to be observed, for the most part they omit it;
as if chance were fitter to be registered than observation. Let diaries therefore be brought in use. The
things to be seen and observed are: the courts of
princes, specially when they give audience to ambassadors; the courts of justice, while they sit and hear
causes; and so of consistories [2] ecclesiastic; the
churches and monasteries, with the monuments which
are therein extant; the walls and fortifications of
cities and towns, and so the havens and harbours;
antiquities and ruins; libraries; colleges, disputations,[3] and lectures, where any are; shipping and
navies; houses and gardens of state and pleasure,

near great cities; armories; arsenals; magazines;
exchanges; burses; warehouses; exercises of horse-
manship, fencing, training of soldiers, and the like;
comedies, such whereunto the better sort of persons
do resort; treasuries of jewels and robes; cabinets and
rarities; and, to conclude, whatsoever is memorable
in the places where they go. After all which the
tutors or servants ought to make diligent inquiry.
As for triumphs, masks, feasts, weddings, funerals,
capital executions, and such shows, men need not
to be put in mind of them; yet they are not to be
neglected. If you will have a young man to put his
travel into a little room, and in short time to gather
much, this you must do. First, as was said, he
must have some entrance into the language before
he goeth. Then he must have such a servant or tutor
as knoweth the country, as was likewise said. Let
him carry with him also some card [4] or book describ-
ing the country where he travelleth; which will be
a good key to his inquiry. Let him keep also a diary.
Let him not stay long in one city or town; more or
less as the place deserveth, but not long; nay, when he
stayeth in one city or town, let him change his
lodging from one end and part of the town to another;
which is a great adamant [5] of acquaintance. Let
him sequester himself from the company of his
countrymen, and diet in such places where there is
good company of the nation where he travelleth.
Let him, upon his removes from one place to another,
procure recommendation to some person of quality
residing in the place whither he removeth, that he
may use his favour in those things he desireth to see
or know. Thus he may abridge his travel with much
profit.

As for the acquaintance which is to be sought in travel, that which is most of all profitable is acquaintance with the secretaries and employed men of ambassadors; for so in travelling in one country he shall suck the experience of many. Let him also see and visit eminent persons in all kinds which are of great name abroad, that he may be able to tell how the life agreeth with the fame. For quarrels, they are with care and discretion to be avoided. They are commonly for mistresses, healths, place, and words. And let a man beware how he keepeth company with choleric and quarrelsome persons, for they will engage him into their own quarrels. When a traveller returneth home, let him not leave the countries where he hath travelled altogether behind him, but maintain a correspondence by letters with those of his acquaintance which are of most worth. And let his travel appear rather in his discourse than in his apparel or gesture; and in his discourse let him be rather advised in his answers than forward to tell stories. And let it appear that he doth not change his country manners [6] for those of foreign parts, but only prick in [7] some flowers of that he hath learned abroad, into the customs of his own country.

OF EXPENSE

RICHES are for spending, and spending for honour and good actions. Therefore extraordinary expense must be limited by the worth of the occasion; for voluntary undoing [1] may be as well for a man's country as for the kingdom of heaven. But ordinary expense ought to be limited by a man's estate; and governed with such regard, as it be within his compass; and

not subject to deceit and abuse of servants; and ordered
to the best show, that the bills may be less than
the estimation abroad. Certainly, if a man will keep
but of even hand, his ordinary expenses ought to be
but to the half of his receipts; and if he think to
wax rich, but to the third part. It is no baseness for
the greatest to descend and look into their own estate.
Some forbear it, not upon negligence alone, but
doubting [2] to bring themselves into melancholy, in
respect they shall find it broken. But wounds cannot be cured without searching. He that cannot
look into his own estate at all, had need both choose
well those whom he employeth, and change them
often; for new are more timorous and less subtle.
He that can look into his estate but seldom, it be-
hooveth him to turn all to certainties.[3] A man had
need, if he be plentiful in some kind of expense, to
be as saving again in some other. As if he be plentiful
in diet, to be saving in apparel; if he be plentiful in
the hall, to be saving in the stable; and the like. For
he that is plentiful in expenses of all kinds will
hardly be preserved from decay. In clearing of
a man's estate, he may as well [4] hurt himself in
being too sudden, as in letting it run on too long.
For hasty selling is commonly as disadvantageable
as interest. Besides, he that clears at once will
relapse; for finding himself out of straits, he will revert to his customs; but he that cleareth by degrees
induceth a habit of frugality, and gaineth as well
upon his mind as upon his estate. Certainly, who hath
a state to repair, may not despise small things; and
commonly it is less dishonourable to abridge petty
charges than to stoop to petty gettings. A man ought
warily to begin charges which once begun will con-

tinue; but in matters that return not he may be
more magnificent.

OF YOUTH AND AGE

A MAN that is young in years may be old in hours,
if he have lost no time. But that happeneth rarely.
Generally youth is like the first cogitations, not so
wise as the second. For there is a youth in thoughts
as well as in ages. And yet the invention of young
men is more lively than that of old; and imaginations stream into their minds better, and, as it
were, more divinely.

Natures that have much heat, and great and violent desires and perturbations, are not ripe for action
till they have passed the meridian of their years;
as it was with Julius Cæsar and Septimius Severus,[1]
of the latter of whom it is said, "Juventutem egit
erroribus, imo furoribus, plenam." [2]   And yet he
was the ablest emperor, almost, of all the list. But
reposed natures may do well in youth, as it is seen
in Augustus Cæsar, Cosmus Duke of Florence,[3]
Gaston de Fois,[4] and others.

On the other side, heat and vivacity in age is an
excellent composition for business. Young men are
fitter to invent than to judge, fitter for execution
than for counsel, and fitter for new projects than for
settled business. For the experience of age, in things
that fall within the compass of it, directeth them,
but in new things abuseth them.

The errors of young men are the ruin of business;
but the errors of aged men amount but to this,— that
more might have been done, or sooner. Young men,
in the conduct and manage of actions, embrace

more than they can hold; stir more than they can
quiet; fly to the end, without consideration of the
means and degrees; pursue some few principles, which
they have chanced upon, absurdly; care not to[5]
innovate, which draws unknown inconveniences;
use extreme remedies at first; and, that which doub-
leth all errors, will not acknowledge or retract them;
like an unready horse, that will neither stop nor turn.

Men of age object too much, consult too long,
adventure too little, repent too soon, and seldom
drive business home to the full period, but content
themselves with a mediocrity of success.

Certainly it is good to compound employments
of both; for that will be good for the present, because
the virtues of either age may correct the defects of
both; and good for succession, that young men may
be learners, while men in age are actors; and, lastly,
good for extern accidents, because authority followeth
old men, and favour and popularity, youth.

But, for the moral part, perhaps, youth will have
the pre-eminence, as age hath for the politic. A
certain Rabbin[6] upon the text, "Your young men
shall see visions, and your old men shall dream
dreams," inferreth that young men are admitted
nearer to God than old, because vision is a clearer
revelation than a dream. And certainly the more
a man drinketh of the world, the more it intoxicateth;
and age doth profit rather in the powers of understanding, than in the virtues of the will and affections.

There be some have an over-early ripeness in their
years, which fadeth betimes. These are, first, such
as have brittle wits, the edge whereof is soon turned;
such as was Hermogenes,[7] the rhetorician, whose
books are exceeding subtile, who afterwards waxed

stupid. A second sort is of those that have some natural dispositions which have better grace in youth
than in age; such as is a fluent and luxuriant speech
which becomes youth well, but not age. So Tully [8]
saith of Hortensius,[9] "Idem manebat, neque idem
decebat." [10] The third is of such as take too high
a strain at the first, and are magnanimous more
than tract of years can uphold; as was Scipio Africanus,[11] of whom Livy [12] saith in effect, "Ultima
primis cedebant." [13]

OF STUDIES

STUDIES serve for delight, for ornament, and
for ability. Their chief use for delight is in privateness and retiring; [1] for ornament, is in discourse;
and for ability, is in the judgment and disposition
of business. For expert men can execute, and perhaps
judge of particulars, one by one; but the general
counsels, and the plots and marshalling of affairs,
come best from those that are learned. To spend
too much time in studies is sloth; to use them too
much for ornament, is affectation; to make judgment wholly by their rules, is the humour of a scholar.
They perfect nature, and are perfected by experience:
for natural abilities are like natural plants, that need
proyning [2] by study; and studies themselves do give
forth directions too much at large, except they be
bounded in by experience. Crafty men contemn
studies, simple men admire them, and wise men use
them; for they teach not their own use; but that is
a wisdom without them, and above them, won
by observation. Read not to contradict and confute;
nor to believe and take for granted; nor to find talk

and discourse; but to weigh and consider. Some books are to be tasted, others to be swallowed, and some few to be chewed and digested; that is, some books are to be read only in parts; others to be read, but not curiously; [3] and some few to be read wholly, and with diligence and attention. Some books also may be read by deputy, and extracts made of them by others; but that would be only in the less important arguments, and the meaner sort of books; else distilled books are like common distilled waters, flashy [4] things. Reading maketh a full man; conference [5] a ready man; and writing an exact man. And therefore, if a man write little, he had need have a great memory; if he confer little, he had need have a present wit; and if he read little, he had need have much cunning, to seem to know that he doth not. Histories make men wise; poets witty; the mathematics subtile; natural philosophy deep; moral grave; logic and rhetoric able to contend. "Abeunt studia in mores." [6] Nay, there is no stone or impediment in the wit but may be wrought out by fit studies; like as diseases of the body may have appropriate exercises. Bowling is good for the stone [7] and reins;[8] shooting for the lungs and breast; gentle walking for the stomach; riding for the head; and the like. So if a man's wit be wandering, let him study the mathematics; for in demonstrations, if his wit be called away never so little, he must begin again. If his wit be not apt to distinguish or find differences, let him study the Schoolmen; for they are *cymini sectores.*[9] If he be not apt to beat over matters, and to call up one thing to prove and illustrate another, let him study the lawyers' cases. So every defect of mind may have a special receipt.

CHARLES LAMB

A DISSERTATION UPON ROAST PIG

MANKIND, says a Chinese manuscript, which my
friend M. [1] was obliging enough to read and explain
to me, for the first seventy thousand ages ate their
meat raw, clawing or biting it from the living animal,
just as they do in Abyssinia to this day. This period
is not obscurely hinted at by their great Confucius [2]
in the second chapter of his Mundane Mutations,
where he designates a kind of golden age by the term
Cho-fang, literally the Cook's holiday. The manuscript goes on to say that the art of roasting, or
rather broiling (which I take to be the elder brother),
was accidentally discovered in the manner following.
The swine-herd, Ho-ti, having gone out into the
woods one morning, as his manner was, to collect
mast for his hogs, left his cottage in the care of his
eldest son, Bo-bo, a great lubberly boy, who being
fond of playing with fire, as younkers of his age commonly are, let some sparks escape into a bundle of
straw, which kindling quickly, spread the confla-
gration over every part of their poor mansion, till
it was reduced to ashes. Together with the cottage
(a sorry antediluvian make-shift of a building, you
may think it), what was of much more importance,
a fine litter of new-farrowed pigs, no less than nine
in number, perished. China pigs have been esteemed a luxury all over the east from the remotest
periods that we read of. Bo-bo was in utmost

consternation, as you may think, not so much for the sake of the tenement, which his father and he could easily build up again with a few dry branches, and the labour of an hour or two, at any time, as for the loss of the pigs. While he was thinking what he should say to his father, and wringing his hands over the smoking remnants of one of those untimely sufferers, an odour assailed his nostrils, unlike any scent which he had before experienced. What could it proceed from? — not from the burnt cottage — he had smelt that smell before — indeed this was by no means the first accident of the kind which had occurred through the negligence of this unlucky young fire-brand. Much less did it resemble that of any known herb, weed, or flower. A premonitory moistening at the same time overflowed his nether lip. He knew not what to think. He next stooped down to feel the pig, if there were any signs of life in it. He burnt his fingers, and to cool them he applied them in his booby fashion to his mouth. Some of the crumbs of the scorched skin had come away with his fingers, and for the first time in his life (in the world's life indeed, for before him no man had known it) he tasted — *crackling!* Again he felt and fumbled at the pig. It did not burn him so much now, still he licked his fingers from a sort of habit. The truth at length broke into his slow understanding, that it was the pig that smelt so, and the pig that tasted so delicious; and, surrendering himself up to the newborn pleasure, he fell to tearing up whole handfuls of the scorched skin with the flesh next it, and was cramming it down his throat in his beastly fashion, when his sire entered amid the smoking rafters, armed with retributory cudgel, and finding how affairs stood, began to rain blows upon the young rogue's shoulders, as thick as hailstones, which Bo-bo heeded not any more than if they had been flies. The tickling pleasure, which he experienced in his lower regions, had rendered him quite callous to any inconveniences he might feel in those remote quarters. His father might lay on, but he could not beat him from his pig, till he had fairly made an end of it, when, becoming a little more sensible of his situation, something like the following dialogue ensued.

"You graceless whelp, what have you got there devouring? Is it not enough that you have burnt me down three houses with your dog's tricks, and be hanged to you, but you must be eating fire, and I know not what — what have you got there, I say?"

"O, father, the pig, the pig, do come and taste how nice the burnt pig eats."

The ears of Ho-ti tingled with horror. He cursed his son, and he cursed himself that ever he should beget a son that should eat burnt pig.

Bo-bo, whose scent was wonderfully sharpened since morning, soon raked out another pig, and fairly rendering it asunder, thrust the lesser half by main force into the fists of Ho-ti, still shouting out, "Eat, eat, eat the burnt pig, father, only taste — O Lord," — with such-like barbarous ejaculations, cramming all the while as if he would choke.

Ho-ti trembled every joint while he grasped the abominable thing, wavering whether he should not put his son to death for an unnatural young monster, when the crackling scorching his fingers, as it had done his son's, and applying the same remedy to them, he in his turn tasted some of its flavour, which, make what sour mouths he would for a pretence, proved not altogether displeasing to him. In conclusion (for the manuscript here is a little tedious) both father and son fairly sat down to the mess, and never left off till they had despatched all that remained of the litter.

Bo-bo was strictly enjoined not to let the secret escape, for the neighbours would certainly have stoned them for a couple of abominable wretches, who could think of improving upon the good meat which God had sent them. Nevertheless strange stories got about. It was observed that Ho-ti's cottage was burnt down now more frequently than ever. Nothing but fires from this time forward. Some would break out in broad day, others in the night-time. As often as the sow farrowed, so sure was the house of Ho-ti to be in a blaze; and Ho-ti himself, which was the more remarkable, instead of chastising his son, seemed to grow more indulgent to him than ever. At length they were watched; the terrible mystery discovered, and father and son summoned to take their trial at Pekin, then an inconsiderable assize town. Evidence was given, the obnoxious food itself produced in court, and verdict about to be pronounced, when the foreman of the jury begged that some of the burnt pig, of which the culprits stood accused, might be handed into the box. He handled it, and they all handled it, and burning their fingers, as Bo-bo and his father had done before them, and Nature prompting to each of them the same remedy, against the face of all the facts, and the clearest charge which judge had ever given,— to the surprise of the whole court, townsfolk, strangers, reporters, and all present — without leaving the box, or any manner of consultation whatever, they brought in a simultaneous verdict of Not Guilty.

The judge, who was a shrewd fellow, winked at the manifest iniquity of the decision; and, when the court was dismissed, went privily, and bought up all the pigs that could be had for love or money. In a few days his Lordship's town house was observed to be on fire. The thing took wing, and now there was nothing to be seen but fires in every direction. Fuel and pigs grew enormously dear all over the district. The insurance offices one and all shut up shop. People built slighter and slighter every day, until it was feared that the very science of architecture would in no long time be lost to the world. Thus this custom of firing houses continued, till in process of time, says my manuscript, a sage arose, like our Locke,[3] who made a discovery, that the flesh of swine, or indeed of any other animal, might be cooked (*burnt*, as they called it) without the necessity of consuming a whole house to dress it. Then first began the rude form of a gridiron. Roasting by the string, or spit, came in a century or two later, I forget in whose dynasty. By such slow degrees, concludes the manuscript, do the most useful, and seemingly the most obvious arts, make their way among mankind.—

Without placing too implicit faith in the account above given, it must be agreed that if a worthy pretext for so dangerous an experiment as setting houses on fire (especially in these days) could be assigned in favor of any culinary object, that pretext and excuse might be found in ROAST PIG.

Of all the delicacies in the whole *mundus edibilis*,[4]

I will maintain it to be the most delicate — *princeps obsoniorum.*[5]

I speak not of your grown porkers — things between pig and pork — those hobbydehoys — but a young and tender suckling — under a moon old — guiltless as yet of the sty — with no original speck of the *amor immunditiæ,*[6] the hereditary failing of the first parent, yet manifest — his voice as yet not broken, but something between a childish treble, and a grumble — the mild forerunner or *præludium,* of a grunt.

He must be roasted. I am not ignorant that our ancestors ate them seethed, or boiled — but what a sacrifice of the exterior tegument!

There is no flavour comparable, I will contend, to that of the crisp, tawny, well-watched, not over-roasted, *crackling,* as it is well called — the very teeth are invited to their share of the pleasure at this banquet in overcoming the coy, brittle resistance — with the adhesive oleaginous — O call it not fat — but an indefinable sweetness growing up to it — the tender blossoming of fat — fat cropped in the bud — taken in the shoot — in the first innocence — the cream and quintessence of the child-pig's yet pure food —— the lean, no lean, but a kind of animal manna — or, rather, fat and lean (if it must be so), so blended and running into each other, that both together make but one ambrosian result, or common substance.

Behold him, while he is doing — it seemeth rather a refreshing warmth, than a scorching heat, that he is so passive to. How equably he twirleth round the string! — Now he is just done. To see the extreme sensibility of that tender age, he hath wept

out his pretty eyes — radiant jellies — shooting
stars —

See him in the dish, his second cradle, how meek he
lieth!— wouldst thou have had this innocent grow
up to the grossness and indocility which too often
accompany maturer swinehood? Ten to one he would
have proved a glutton, a sloven, an obstinate, disagreeable animal — wallowing in all manner of
filthy conversation — from these sins he is happily
snatched away —

> Ere sin could blight, or sorrow fade,
> Death came with timely care —[7]

his memory is odoriferous — no clown curseth, while
his stomach half rejecteth, the rank bacon — no
coal-heaver bolteth him in reeking sausages — he
hath a fair sepulchre in the grateful stomach of the
judicious epicure — and for such a tomb might be
content to die.

He is the best of Sapors. Pine-apple is great. She
is indeed almost too transcendent — a delight, if
not sinful, yet so like to sinning, that really a tender-
conscienced person would do well to pause — too
ravishing for mortal taste, she woundeth and ex-
coriateth the lips that approach her — like lovers'
kisses, she biteth — she is a pleasure bordering on
pain from the fierceness and insanity of her relish
— but she stoppeth at the palate — she meddleth
not with the appetite — and the coarsest hunger
might barter her consistently for a mutton chop.

Pig — let me speak his praise — is no less provoc-
ative of the appetite, than he is satisfactory to the
criticalness of the censorious palate. The strong man

may batten on him, and weakling refuseth not his mild juices.

Unlike to mankind's mixed characters, a bundle of virtues and vices, inexplicably intertwisted, and not to be unravelled without hazard, he is — good throughout. No part of him is better or worse than another. He helpeth, as far as his little means extend, all around. He is the least envious of banquets. He is all neighbours' fare.

I am one of those who freely and ungrudgingly impart a share of the good things of this life which fall to their lot (few as mine are in this kind) to a friend. I protest I take as great an interest in my friend's pleasures, his relishes, and proper satisfactions, as in mine own. "Presents," I often say, "endear Absents." Hares, pheasants, partridges, snipes, barn-door chickens (those "tame vilatic fowl"), capons, plovers, brawn, barrels of oysters, I dispense as freely as I receive them. I love to taste them, as it were, upon the tongue of my friend. But a stop must be put somewhere. One would not, like Lear, "give everything." I make stand upon pig. Methinks it is an ingratitude to the Giver of all good flavours, to extra-domiciliate, or send out of the house, slightingly (under pretext of friendship, or I know not what), a blessing so particularly adapted, predestined, I may say, to my individual palate — it argues an insensibility.

I remember a touch of conscience in this kind at school. My good old aunt, who never parted from me at the end of a holiday without stuffing a sweetmeat, or some nice thing, into my pocket, had dismissed me one evening with a smoking plum-cake, fresh from the oven. In my way to school (it was over

London bridge) a grey-headed old beggar saluted me (I have no doubt at this time of day that he was a counterfeit). I had no pence to console him with, and in the vanity of self-denial, and the very coxcombry of charity, school-boy like, I made him a present of — the whole cake. I walked on a little, buoyed up, as one is on such occasions, with a sweet soothing of self-satisfaction; but before I had got to the end of the bridge, my better feelings returned, and I burst into tears, thinking how ungrateful I had been to my good aunt, to go and give her good gift away to a stranger, that I had never seen before, and who might be a bad man for aught I knew; and then I thought of the pleasure my aunt would be taking in thinking that I — I myself, and not another — would eat her nice cake — and what should I say to her the next time I saw her — how naughty I was to part with her pretty present — and the odour of that spicy cake came back upon my recollection, and the pleasure and the curiosity I had taken in seeing her make it, and her joy when she sent it to the oven, and how disappointed she would feel that I had never had a bit of it in my mouth at last — and I blamed my impertinent spirit of alms-giving, and out-of-place hypocrisy of goodness, and above all I wished never to see the face again of that insiduous, good-for-nothing, old grey imposter.

Our ancestors were nice in their method of sacrificing these tender victims. We read of pigs whipt to death with something of a shock, as we hear of any other obsolete custom. The age of discipline is gone by, or it would be curious to inquire (in a philosophical light merely) what effect this process might have towards intenerating and dulcifying a

substance, naturally so mild and dulcet as the flesh
of young pigs. It looks like refining a violet. Yet we
should be cautious, while we condemn the inhuman-
ity, how we censure the wisdom of the practice. It
might impart a gusto —

I remember an hypothesis, argued upon by the
young students, when I was at St. Omer's,[8] and
maintained with much learning and pleasantry on
both sides, "Whether, supposing that the flavour
of a pig who obtained his death by whipping (*per
flagellationem extremam*) [9] superadded a pleasure upon
the palate of a man more intense than any possible
suffering we can conceive in the animal, is man justified in using that method of putting the animal to
death?" I forget the decision.

His sauce should be considered. Decidedly, a few
bread crumbs, done up with his liver and brains, and
a dash of mild sage. But banish, dear Mrs. Cook, I
beseech you, the whole onion tribe. Barbecue
your whole hogs to your palate, steep them in shalots,
stuff them out with plantations of the rank and
guilty garlic; you cannot poison them, or make them
stronger than they are — but consider, he is a weakling — a flower.

POOR RELATIONS

A POOR RELATION — is the most irrelevant thing
in nature, — a piece of impertinent correspondency —
an odious approximation,— a haunting conscience,
— a preposterous shadow, lengthening in the noon-
tide of our prosperity,— an unwelcome remembrancer,
— a perpetually recurring mortification,— a drain
on your purse,— a more intolerable dun upon your

pride,— a drawback upon success,— a rebuke to
your rising,— a stain in your blood,— a blot on your
'scutcheon,— a rent in your garment,— a death's
head at your banquet,— Agathocles' pot,[1]— a Mordecai in your gate,[2]— a Lazarus at your door,— a
lion in your path,— a frog in your chamber,— a
fly in your ointment,— a mote in your eye,— a
triumph to your enemy, an apology to your friends,
— the one thing not needful,— the hail in harvest,
— the ounce of sour in a pound of sweet.

He is known by his knock. Your heart telleth you
"That is Mr.——." A rap, between familiarity and
respect; that demands, and, at the same time, seems
to despair of, entertainment. He entereth smiling
and — embarrassed. He holdeth out his hand to
you to shake, and — draweth it back again. He casually looketh in about dinner-time — when the table
is full. He offereth to go away, seeing you have company, but is induced to stay. He filleth a chair,
and your visitor's two children are accommodated at
a side table. He never cometh upon open days, when
your wife says with some complacency, "My dear,
perhaps Mr.—— will drop in to-day." He remem-
bereth birthdays — and professeth he is fortunate
to have stumbled upon one. He declareth against
fish, the turbot being small — yet suffereth himself
to be importuned into a slice against his first resolution. He sticketh by the port — yet will be prevailed upon to empty the remainder glass of claret, if
a stranger press it upon him. He is a puzzle to the
servants, who are fearful of being too obsequious,
or not civil enough, to him. The guests think "they
have seen him before." Every one speculateth
upon his condition; and the most part take him to

be — a tide waiter. He calleth you by your Christian name, to imply that his other is the same with your own. He is too familiar by half, yet you wish he had less diffidence. With half the familiarity he might pass for a casual dependent; with more boldness he would be in no danger of being taken for what he is. He is too humble for a friend, yet taketh on him more state than befits a client. He is a worse guest than a country tenant, inasmuch as he bringeth up no rent — yet 'tis odds, from his garb and demeanour, that your guests take him for one. He is asked to make one at the whist table; refuseth on the score of poverty, and — resents being left out. When the company break up he proffereth to go for a coach — and lets the servants go. He recollects your grandfather; and will thrust in some mean and quite unimportant anecdote of — the family. He knew it when it was not quite so flourishing as "he is blest in seeing it now." He reviveth past situations to institute what he calleth — favourable comparisons. With a reflecting sort of congratulation, he will inquire the price of your furniture: and insults you with a special commendation of your window-curtains. He is of opinion that the urn is the more elegant shape, but, after all, there was something more comfortable about the old tea-kettle — which you must remember. He dare say you must find a great convenience in having a carriage of your own, and appealeth to your lady if it is not so. Inquireth if you have had your arms done on vellum yet; and did not know, till lately, that such-and-such had been the crest of the family. His memory is unseasonable; his compliments perverse; his talk a trouble; his stay pertinacious; and when he goeth away, you

dismiss his chair into a corner, as precipitately as possible, and feel fairly rid of two nuisances.

There is a worse evil under the sun, and that is
— a female Poor Relation. You may do something
with the other; you may pass him off tolerably well;
but your indigent she-relative is hopeless. "He is an
old humorist," you may say, "and affects to go
threadbare. His circumstances are better than folks
would take them to be. You are fond of having a
Character at your table, and truly he is one." But
in the indications of female poverty there can be no
disguise. No woman dresses below herself from ca-
price. The truth must out without shuffling. "She
is plainly related to the L——s; or what does she
at their house?" She is, in all probability, your wife's
cousin. Nine times out of ten, at least, this is the
case. Her garb is something between a gentlewoman
and a beggar, yet the former evidently predominates.
She is most provokingly humble, and ostentatiously
sensible to her inferiority. He may require to be
repressed sometimes — *aliquando sufflaminandus erat* [3]
— but there is no raising her. You send her soup
at dinner, and she begs to be helped — after the
gentlemen. Mr.—— requests the honour of taking
wine with her; she hesitates between Port and Ma-
deira, and chooses the former — because he does.
She calls the servant *Sir;* and insists on not troubling
him to hold her plate. The housekeeper patronizes
her. The children's governess takes upon her to
correct her, when she has mistaken the piano for
harpsichord.

Richard Amlet, Esq.,[4] in the play, is a noticeable
instance of the disadvantages to which this chimerical
notion of *affinity constituting a claim to an acquain-*

tance, may subject the spirit of a gentleman. A little
foolish blood is all that is betwixt him and a lady
with a great estate. His stars are perpetually crossed
by the malignant maternity of an old woman, who
persists in calling him "her son Dick." But she
has wherewithal in the end to recompense his indig-
nities, and float him again upon the brilliant surface,
under which it had been her seeming business and
pleasure all along to sink him. All men, besides, are
not of Dick's temperament. I knew an Amlet in
real life, who wanting Dick's buoyancy, sank indeed.
Poor W——[5] was of my own standing at Christ's,
a fine classic, and a youth of promise. If he had a
blemish, it was too much pride; but its quality was
inoffensive; it was not of that sort which hardens
the heart, and serves to keep inferiors at a distance;
it only sought to ward off derogation from itself.
It was the principle of self-respect carried as far
as it could go, without infringing on that respect,
which he would have every one else equally maintain
for himself. He would have you think alike with him
on this topic. Many a quarrel have I had with him,
when we were rather older boys, and our tallness
made us more obnoxious to observation in the blue
clothes, because I would not thread the alleys and
blind ways of the town with him to elude notice, when
we have been out together on a holiday in the streets
of this sneering and prying metropolis. W——
went, sore with these notions, to Oxford, where the
dignity and sweetness of a scholar's life, meeting with
the alloy of a humble introduction, wrought in
him a passionate devotion to the place, with a profound aversion to the society. The servitor's gown
(worse than his school array) clung to him with Nes-

sian venom.[6] He thought himself ridiculous in a
garb, under which Latimer [7] must have walked erect;
and in which Hooker,[8] in his young days, possibly
flaunted in a vein of no discommendable vanity.
In the depths of college shades, or in his lonely chamber, the poor student shrunk from observation.
He found shelter among books, which insult not;
and studies, that ask no questions of a youth's
finances. He was lord of his library, and seldom cared
for looking out beyond his domains. The healing
influence of studious pursuits was upon him, to soothe
and to abstract. He was almost a healthy man;
when the waywardness of his fate broke out against
him with a second and worse malignity. The father
of W—— had hitherto exercised the humble profession of house-painter at N——, near Oxford. A supposed interest with some of the heads of colleges
had now induced him to take up his abode in that
city, with the hope of being employed upon some
public works which were talked of. From that
moment I read in the countenance of the young man,
the determination which at length tore him from
academical pursuits for ever. To a person unac-
quainted with our Universities, the distance between
the gownsmen and the townsmen, as they are called
— the trading part of the latter especially — is carried
to an excess that would appear harsh and incredible.
The temperament of W——'s father was diametrically
the reverse of his own. Old W—— was a little, busy,
cringing tradesman, who, with his son upon his arm,
would stand bowing and scraping, cap in hand, to
anything that wore the semblance of a gown — insensible to the winks and opener remonstrances of the
young man, to whose chamber-fellow, or equal in

standing, perhaps, he was thus obsequiously and gratuitously ducking. Such a state of things could not last. W—— must change the air of Oxford or be suffocated. He chose the former; and let the sturdy moralist, who strains the point of the filial duties as high as they can bear, censure the dereliction; he cannot estimate the struggle. I stood with W——, the last afternoon I ever saw him, under the eaves of his paternal dwelling. It was in the fine lane leading from the High Street to the back of . . . college, where W—— kept his rooms. He seemed thoughtful, and more reconciled. I ventured to rally him — finding him in a better mood — upon a representation of the Artist Evangelist,[9] which the old man, whose affairs were beginning to flourish, had caused to be set up in a splendid sort of frame over his really handsome shop, either as a token of prosperity, or badge of gratitude to his saint. W—— looked up at the Luke, and, like Satan, "knew his mounted sign — and fled." A letter on his father's table the next morning, announced that he had accepted a commission in a regiment about to embark for Portugal. He was among the first who perished before the walls of St. Sebastian.[10]

I do not know how, upon a subject which I began with treating half seriously, I should have fallen upon a recital so eminently painful; but this theme of poor relationship is replete with so much matter for tragic as well as comic associations, that it is difficult to keep the account distinct without blending. The earliest impressions which I received on this matter, are certainly not attended with anything painful, or very humiliating, in the recalling. At my father's table (no very splendid one) was to be found,

every Saturday the mysterious figure of an aged
gentleman, clothed in neat black, of a sad yet comely
appearance. His deportment was of the essence of
gravity; his words few or none; and I was not to
make a noise in his presence. I had little inclination
to have done so — for my cue was to admire in
silence. A particular elbow chair was appropriated
to him, which was in no case to be violated. A
peculiar sort of sweet pudding, which appeared on
no other occasion, distinguished the days of his
coming. I used to think him a prodigiously rich
man. All I could make out of him was, that he and
my father had been school-fellows a world ago at
Lincoln, and that he came from the Mint. The
Mint I knew to be a place where all the money was
coined — and I thought he was the owner of all that
money. Awful ideas of the Tower twined themselves
about his presence. He seemed above human in-
firmities and passions. A sort of melancholy grandeur
invested him. From some inexplicable doom I fancied him obliged to go about in an eternal suit of
mourning; a captive — a stately being, let out of the
Tower on Saturdays. Often have I wondered at
the temerity of my father, who, in spite of an habitual general respect which we all in common mani-
fested towards him, would venture now and then to
stand up against him in some argument, touching
their youthful days. The houses of the ancient city
of Lincoln are divided (as most of my readers know)
between the dwellers on the hill, and in the valley.
This marked distinction formed an obvious division
between the boys who lived above (however brought
together in a common school) and the boys whose
paternal residence was on the plain; a sufficient cause

of hostility in the code of these young Grotiuses.[11]
My father had been a leading Mountaineer; and would
still maintain the general superiority, in skill and
hardihood, of the *Above Boys* (his own faction)
over the *Below Boys* (so were they called), of which
party his contemporary had been a chieftain. Many
and hot were the skirmishes on this topic — the only
one upon which the old gentleman was ever brought
out — and bad blood bred; even sometimes almost
to the recommencement (so I expected) of actual
hostilities. But my father, who scorned to insist
upon advantages, generally contrived to turn the
conversation upon some adroit by-commendation
of the old Minster; in the general preference of which,
before all other cathedrals in the island, the dweller
on the hill, and the plain-born, could meet on a con-
ciliating level, and lay down their less important
differences. Once only I saw the old gentleman really
ruffled, and I remembered with anguish the thought
that came over me: "Perhaps he will never come here
again." He had been pressed to take another plate
of the viand, which I have already mentioned as the
indispensable concomitant of his visits. He had
refused with a resistance amounting to rigour, when
my aunt — an old Lincolnian, but who had something
of this in common with my cousin Bridget, that she
would sometimes press civility out of season —
uttered the following memorable application —
"Do take another slice, Mr. Billet, for you do not
get pudding every day." The old gentleman said
nothing at the time — but he took occasion in the
course of the evening, when some argument had intervened between them, to utter an emphasis which
chilled the company, and which chills me now as

I write it — "Woman, you are superannuated."
John Billet did not survive long, after the digesting
of this affront; but he survived long enough to as-
sure me that peace was actually restored and, if I
remember aright, another pudding was discreetly
substituted in place of that which had occasioned the
offence. He died at the Mint (anno 1781) where he
had long held, what he accounted, a comfortable
independence; and with five pounds, fourteen shill-
ings, and a penny, which were found in his escri-
toire after his decease, left the world, blessing God
that he had enough to bury him, and that he had never
been obliged to any man for a sixpence. This was
— a Poor Relation.

THE SUPERANNUATED MAN

> Sera tamen respexit
> Libertas. VIRGIL.[1]
> A Clerk I was in London gay.
> O'KEEFE.[2]

IF peradventure, Reader, it has been thy lot to
waste the golden years of thy life — thy shining youth
— in the irksome confinement of an office; to have thy
prison days prolonged through middle age down to
decrepitude and silver hairs, without hope of release
or respite; to have lived to forget that there are such
things as holydays, or to remember them but as the
prerogatives of childhood; then, and then only, will
you be able to appreciate my deliverance.

It is now six and thirty years since I took my seat
at the desk in Mincing Lane. Melancholy was the
transition at fourteen from the abundant playtime,
and the frequently intervening vacations of school

days, to the eight, nine, and sometimes ten hours'
a-day attendance at a counting-house. But time
partially reconciles us to anything. I gradually
became content — doggedly content, as wild animals
in cages.

It is true I had my Sundays to myself; but Sundays, admirable as the institution of them is for
purposes of worship, are for that very reason the
very worst adapted for days of unbending and rec-
reation. In particular, there is a gloom for me atten-
dant upon a city Sunday, a weight in the air. I miss
the cheerful cries of London, the music, and the ballad-
singers — the buzz and stirring murmur of the streets.
Those eternal bells depress me. The closed shops
repel me. Prints, pictures, all the glittering and endless succession of knacks and gewgaws, and ostentatiously displayed wares of tradesmen, which make a
week-day saunter through the less busy parts of the
metropolis so delightful — are shut out. No book-
stalls deliciously to idle over. No busy faces to recreate the idle man who contemplates them ever
passing by — the very face of business a charm by
contrast to his temporary relaxation from it. Nothing
to be seen but unhappy countenances — or half-
happy at best — of emancipated 'prentices and little
tradesfolks, with here and there a servant maid that
has got leave to go out, who, slaving all the week,
with the habit has lost almost the capacity of en-
joying a free hour; and livelily expressing the hollowness of a day's pleasuring. The very strollers
in the fields on that day looked anything but
comfortable.

But besides Sundays I had a day at Easter, and a
day at Christmas, with a full week in the summer to

go and air myself in my native fields of Hertford-
shire. This last was a great indulgence; and the
prospect of its recurrence, I believe, alone kept me
up through the year, and made my durance tolerable. But when the week came round, did the glittering phantom of the distance keep touch with me?
or rather was it not a series of seven uneasy days,
spent in restless pursuit of pleasure, and a wearisome
anxiety to find out how to make the most of them?
Where was the quiet, where the promised rest?
Before I had a taste of it, it was vanished. I was at
the desk again, counting upon the fifty-one tedious
weeks that must intervene before such another snatch
would come. Still the prospect of its coming threw
something of an illumination upon the darker side
of my captivity. Without it, as I have said, I could
scarcely have sustained my thraldom.

Independently of the rigours of attendance, I have
ever been haunted with a sense (perhaps a mere ca-
price) of incapacity for business. This, during my
latter years, had increased to such a degree, that it
was visible in all the lines of my countenance. My
health and my good spirits flagged. I had perpetually a dread of some crisis, to which I should
be found unequal. Besides my daylight servitude,
I served over again all night in my sleep, and would
awake with terrors of imaginary false entries, errors
in my accounts, and the like. I was fifty years of
age, and no prospect of emancipation presented
itself. I had grown to my desk, as it were; and the
wood had entered my soul.

My fellows in the office would sometimes rally me
upon the trouble legible in my countenance; but I
did not know that it had raised the suspicions of any

of my employers, when on the 5th of last month, a day ever to be remembered by me, L——,[3] the junior partner in the firm, calling me on one side, directly taxed me with my bad looks, and frankly inquired the cause of them. So taxed, I honestly made confession of my infirmity, and added that I was afraid I should eventually be obliged to resign his service. He spoke some words of course to hearten me, and there the matter rested. A whole week I remained labouring under the impression that I had acted imprudently in my disclosure; that I had foolishly given a handle against myself, and had been anticipating my own dismissal. A week passed in this manner, the most anxious one, I verily believe, in my whole life, when on the evening of the 12th of April, just as I was about quitting my desk to go home (it might be about eight o'clock) I received an awful summons to attend the presence of the whole assembled firm in the formidable back parlour. I thought now my time is surely come, I have done for myself, I am going to be told that they have no longer occasion for me. L——, I could see, smiled at the terror I was in, which was a little relief to me,— when to my utter astonishment B——,[4] the eldest partner, began a formal harangue to me on the length of my services, my very meritorious conduct during the whole of that time (the deuce, thought I, how did he find out that? I protest I never had the confidence to think as much). He went on to descant on the expediency of retiring at a certain time of life (how my heart panted!), and asking me a few questions as to the amount of my own property, of which I have a little, ended with a proposal, to which his three partners nodded a grave assent, that I should accept from the house, which I had served so well, a pension for life to the amount of two-thirds of my accustomed salary — a magnificent offer. I do not know what I answered between surprise and gratitude, but it was understood that I accepted their proposal, and I was told that I was free from that hour to leave their service. I stammered out a bow, and at just ten minutes after eight I went home — for ever. This noble benefit — gratitude forbids me to conceal their names — I owe to the kindness of the most munificent firm in the world —the house of Boldero, Merryweather, Bosanquet, and Lacy.[5]

Esto perpetua![6]

For the first day or two I felt stunned, overwhelmed. I could only apprehend my felicity; I was too confused to taste it sincerely. I wandered about, thinking I was happy, and knowing that I was not. I was in the condition of a prisoner in the Old Bastile,[7] suddenly let loose after a forty years' confinement. I could scarce trust myself with myself. It was like passing out of Time into Eternity — for it is a sort of Eternity for a man to have his Time all to himself. It seemed to me that I had more time on my hands than I could ever manage. From a poor man, poor in Time, I was suddenly lifted up into a vast revenue; I could see no end of my possessions; I wanted some steward, or judicious bailiff, to manage my estates in Time for me. And here let me caution persons grown old in active business, not lightly, nor without weighing their own resources, to forego their customary employment all at once, for there may be danger in it. I feel

it by myself, but I know that my resources are
sufficient; and now that those first giddy raptures
have subsided, I have a quiet home-feeling of the
blessedness of my condition. I am in no hurry.
Having all holydays, I am as though I had none.
If Time hung heavy upon me, I could walk it away;
but I do *not* walk all day long, as I used to do in those
old transient holydays, thirty miles a day, to make the
most of them. If Time were troublesome, I could
read it away, but I do *not* read in that violent measure,
with which, having no Time my own but candle-
light Time, I used to weary out my head and eyesight in by-gone winters. I walk, read, or scribble
(as now) just when the fit seizes me. I no longer
hunt after pleasure; I let it come to me. I am like
the man

————that's born, and has his years come to him,
In some green desert.[8]

"Years," you will say; "what is this superannuated
simpleton calculating upon? He has already told
he is past fifty."

I have indeed lived nominally fifty years, but de-
duct out of them the hours which I have lived to
other people, and not to myself, and you will find me
still a young fellow. For *that* is the only true Time,
which a man can properly call his own, that which
he has all to himself; the rest, though in some sense
he may be said to live it, is other people's time, not
his. The remnant of my poor days, long or short, is
at least multiplied for me threefold. My ten next
years, if I stretch so far, will be as long as any preceding thirty. 'T is a fair rule-of-three sum.

Among the strange fantasies which beset me at the
commencement of my freedom, and of which all

traces are not yet gone, one was, that a vast tract of time had intervened since I quitted the Counting House. I could not conceive of it as an affair of yesterday. The partners, and the clerks with whom I had for so many years, and for so many hours in each day of the year been so closely associated — being suddenly removed from them — they seemed as dead to me. There is a fine passage, which may serve to illustrate this fancy, in a Tragedy, by Sir Robert Howard, speaking of a friend's death:—

> ———'T was but just now he went away;
> I have not since had time to shed a tear;
> And yet the distance does the same appear
> As if he had been a thousand years from me.
> Time takes no measure in Eternity.[9]

To dissipate this awkward feeling, I have been fain to go among them once or twice since; to visit my old desk-fellows — my co-brethren of the quill — that I had left below in the state militant. Not all the kindness with which they received me could quite restore to me that pleasant familiarity which I had heretofore enjoyed among them. We cracked some of our old jokes, but methought they went off but faintly. My old desk; the peg where I hung my hat, were appropriated to another. I knew it must be, but I could not take it kindly. D——l take me if I did not feel some remorse — beast, if I had not — at quitting my old compeers, the faithful partners of my toils for six and thirty years, that smoothed for me with their jokes and conundrums the ruggedness of my professional road. Had it been so rugged then after all? or was I a coward simply? Well, it is too late to repent; and I also know, that these suggestions are a common fallacy of the mind

on such occasions. But my heart smote me. I
had violently broken the bonds betwixt us. It was at
least not courteous. I shall be some time before
I get quite reconciled to the separation. Farewell,
old cronies, yet not for long, for again and again I will
come among ye, if I shall have your leave. Farewell,
Ch——, dry, sarcastic, and friendly! Do——, mild,
slow to move, and gentlemanly! Pl——, officious to
do, and to volunteer good services!—— and thou,
thou dreary pile, fit mansion for a Gresham [10] or a
Whittington [11] of old stately House of Merchants;
with thy labyrinthine passages, and light-excluding,
pent-up offices, where candles for one half the year
supplied the place of the sun's light; unhealthy contributor to my weal, stern fosterer of my living, farewell! In thee remain, and not in the obscure collection of some wandering bookseller, my "works!"
There let them rest, as I do from my labours, piled
on thy massy shelves, more MSS. in folio than ever
Aquinas [12] left, and full as useful! My mantle I
bequeath among ye.

A fortnight has passed since the date of my first
communication. At that period I was approaching
to tranquillity, but had not reached it. I boasted
of a calm indeed, but it was comparative only.
Something of the first flutter was left; an unset-
tling sense of novelty; the dazzle to weak eyes of
unaccustomed light. I missed my old chains, for-
sooth, as if they had been some necessary part of
my apparel. I was a poor Carthusian,[13] from strict
cellular discipline suddenly by some revolution returned upon the world. I am now as if I had never
been other than my own master. It is natural to me
to go where I please, to do what I please. I find

myself at eleven o'clock in the day in Bond Street, and
it seems to me that I have been sauntering there
at that very hour for years past. I digress into
Soho, to explore a book-stall. Methinks I have been
thirty years a collector. There is nothing strange
nor new in it. I find myself before a fine picture
in the morning. Was it ever otherwise? What
is become of Fish Street Hill? Where is Fenchurch
Street? Stones of old Mincing Lane which I have
worn with my daily pilgrimage for six and thirty years,
to the footsteps of what toil-worn clerk are your everlasting flints now vocal? I indent the gayer flags
of Pall Mall. It is 'Change time, and I am strangely
among the Elgin marbles.[14] It was no hyperbole
when I ventured to compare the change in my condition to a passing into another world. Time stands
still in a manner to me. I have lost all distinction
of season. I do not know the day of the week, or of
the month. Each day used to be individually felt
by me in its reference to the foreign post days; in
its distance from, or propinquity to the next Sunday.
I had my Wednesday feelings, my Saturday nights'
sensations. The genius of each day was upon me distinctly during the whole of it, affecting my appetite,
spirits, &c. The phantom of the next day, with the
dreary five to follow, sate as a load upon my poor
Sabbath recreations. What charm has washed the
Ethiop white? What is gone of Black Monday?
All days are the same. Sunday itself — that unfortunate failure of a holiday as it too often proved,
what with my sense of its fugitiveness, and over-care
to get the greatest quantity of pleasure out of it—
is melted down into a week day. I can spare to go
to church now, without grudging the huge cantle

which it used to seem to cut out of the holyday.
I have Time for everything. I can visit a sick friend.
I can interrupt the man of much occupation when he is
busiest. I can insult over him with an invitation to
take a day's pleasure with me to Windsor this fine
May-morning. It is Lucretian pleasure to behold
the poor drudges, whom I have left behind in the
world, carking and caring; like horses in a mill,
drudging on in the same eternal round — and what
is it all for? A man can never have too much Time
to himself, nor too little to do. Had I a little son,
I would christen him NOTHING-TO-DO; he should
do nothing. Man, I verily believe, is out of his element
as long as he is operative. I am altogether for the
life contemplative. Will no kindly earthquake
come and swallow up those accursed cotton mills?
Take me that lumber of a desk there, and bowl it
down

As low as to the fiends.

I am no longer . . . , clerk to the firm of, &c. I
am Retired Leisure. I am to be met with in trim
gardens. I am already come to be known by my
vacant face and careless gesture, perambulating at
no fixed pace nor with any settled purpose. I walk
about; not to and from. They tell me, a certain *cum
dignitate* [15] air, that has been buried so long with
my other good parts, has begun to shoot forth in my
person. I grow into gentility perceptibly. When I
take up a newspaper it is to read the state of the
opera. *Opus operatum est.* [16] I have done all that I
came into this world to do. I have worked task-work,
and have the rest of the day to myself.

WILLIAM HAZLITT

ON GOING A JOURNEY

ONE of the pleasantest things in the world is going a journey; but I like to go by myself. I can enjoy society in a room; but out of doors, nature is company enough for me. I am then never less alone than when alone.

> "The fields his study, nature was his book."

I cannot see the wit of walking and talking at the same time. When I am in the country, I wish to vegetate like the country. I am not for criticising hedge-rows and black cattle. I go out of town in order to forget the town and all that is in it. There are those who for this purpose go to watering-places, and carry the metropolis with them. I like more elbow-room, and fewer incumbrances. I like solitude, when I give myself up to it, for the sake of solitude; nor do I ask for

> "a friend in my retreat,
> Whom I may whisper solitude is sweet."

The soul of a journey is liberty, perfect liberty, to think, feel, do just as one pleases. We go a journey chiefly to be free of all impediments and of all inconveniences; to leave ourselves behind, much more to get rid of others. It is because I want a little breathing space to muse on indifferent matters, where Contemplation

"May plume her feathers and let grow her wings,
That in the various bustle of resort
Were all too-ruffled, and sometimes impair'd,"

that I absent myself from the town for a while, without feeling at a loss the moment I am left by myself. Instead of a friend in a post-chaise or in a Tilbury, to exchange good things with, and vary the same stale topics over again, for once let me have a truce with impertinence. Give me the clear blue sky over my head, and the green turf beneath my feet, a winding road before me, and a three hours' march to dinner — and then to thinking. It is hard if I cannot start some game on these lone heaths. I laugh, I run, I leap, I sing for joy. From the point of yonder rolling cloud, I plunge into my past being, and revel there, as the sun-burnt Indian plunges headlong into the wave that wafts him to his native shore. Then long-forgotten things, like "sunken wrack and sumless treasuries," burst upon my eager sight, and I begin to feel, think, and be myself again. Instead of an awkward silence, broken by attempts at wit or dull commonplaces, mine is that undisturbed silence of the heart which alone is perfect eloquence. No one likes puns, alliterations, antitheses, argument, and analysis better than I do; but I sometimes had rather be without them. "Leave, oh, leave me to my repose!" I have just now other business in hand, which would seem idle to you, but is with me "very stuff of the conscience." Is not this wild rose sweet without a comment? Does not this daisy leap to my heart set in its coat of emerald? Yet if I were to explain to you the circumstance that has so endeared it to me, you would only smile. Had I not better then keep it to myself, and let it serve me to brood over, from here to yonder craggy point, and from thence onward to the far-distant horizon? I should be but bad company all that way, and therefore prefer being alone. I have heard it said that you may, when the moody fit comes on, walk or ride on by yourself, and indulge your reveries. But this looks like a breach of manners, a neglect of others, and you are thinking all the time that you ought to rejoin your party. "Out upon such half-faced fellowship," say I. I like to be either entirely to myself, or entirely at the disposal of others; to talk or be silent, to walk or sit still, to be sociable or solitary. I was pleased with an observation of Mr. Cobbett's,[1] that "he thought it a bad French custom to drink our wine with our meals, and that an Englishman ought to do only one thing at a time." So I cannot talk and think, or indulge in melancholy musing and lively conversation by fits and starts. "Let me have a companion of my way," says Sterne,[2] "were it but to remark how the shadows lengthen as the sun declines." It is beautifully said: but in my opinion, this continual comparing of notes interferes with the involuntary impression of things upon the mind, and hurts the sentiment. If you only hint what you feel in a kind of dumb show, it is insipid: if you have to explain it, it is making a toil of a pleasure. You cannot read the book of nature, without being perpetually put to the trouble of translating it for the benefit of others. I am for the synthetical method on a journey, in preference to the analytical. I am content to lay in a stock of ideas then, and to examine and anatomize them afterwards. I want to see my vague notions float like the down of the thistle before the breeze, and not to have them entangled in the briars and thorns of contro-

versy. For once, I like to have it all my own way;
and this is impossible unless you are alone, or in such
company as I do not covet. I have no objection to
argue a point with any one for twenty miles of measured road, but not for pleasure. If you remark
the scent of a beanfield crossing the road, perhaps
your fellow-traveller has no smell. If you point to
a distant object, perhaps he is short-sighted, and has
to take out his glass to look at it. There is a feeling
in the air, a tone in the colour of a cloud which hits
your fancy, but the effect of which you are unable to
account for. There is then no sympathy, but an
uneasy craving after it, and a dissatisfaction which
pursues you on the way, and in the end probably
produces ill humour. Now I never quarrel with myself, and take all my own conclusions for granted till
I find it necessary to defend them against objec-
tions. It is not merely that you may not be of accord
on the objects and circumstances that present themselves before you — these may recall a number
of objects, and lead to associations too delicate and
refined to be possibly communicated to others. Yet
these I love to cherish, and sometimes still fondly
clutch them, when I can escape from the throng to
do so. To give way to our feelings before company
seems extravagance or affectation; and on the other
hand, to have to unravel this mystery of our being at
every turn, and to make others take an equal interest
in it (otherwise the end is not answered) is a task to
which few are competent. We must "give it an understanding, but no tongue." My old friend C——,[3]
however, could do both. He could go on in the most
delightful explanatory way over hill and dale, a
summer's day, and convert a landscape into a didac-

tic poem or a Pindaric ode. "He talked far above singing." If I could so clothe my ideas in sounding and flowing words, I might perhaps wish to have some one with me to admire the swelling theme; or I could be more content, were it possible for me still to hear his echoing voice in the woods of All-Foxden. They had "that fine madness in them which our first poets had;" and if they could have been caught by some rare instrument, would have breathed such strains as the following: —

> "Here be woods as green
> As any, air likewise as fresh and sweet
> As when smooth Zephyrus plays on the fleet
> Face of the curled stream, with flow'rs as many
> As the young spring gives, and as choice as any;
> Here be all new delights, cool streams and wells,
> Arbours o'ergrown with woodbine, caves and dells;
> Choose where thou wilt, while I sit by and sing,
> Or gather rushes to make many a ring
> For thy long fingers; tell thee tales of love,
> How the pale Phoebe, hunting in a grove,
> First saw the boy Endymion, from whose eyes
> She took eternal fire that never dies;
> How she convey'd him softly in a sleep,
> His temples bound with poppy, to the steep
> Head of old Latmos, where she stoops each night,
> Gilding the mountain with her brother's light,
> To kiss her sweetest."
>
> *Faithful Shepherdess.*

Had I words and images at command like these, I would attempt to wake the thoughts that lie slumbering on golden ridges in the evening clouds: but at the sight of nature my fancy, poor as it is, droops and closes up its leaves, like flowers at sunset. I can make nothing out on the spot: — I must have time to collect myself.

In general, a good thing spoils out-of-door prospects:
it should be reserved for Table-talk. L——⁴ is for
this reason, I take it, the worst company in the world
out of doors; because he is the best within. I grant,
there is one subject on which it is pleasant to talk
on a journey; and that is, what one shall have for
supper when we get to our inn at night. The open
air improves this sort of conversation or friendly
altercation, by setting a keener edge on appetite.
Every mile of the road heightens the flavour of the
viands we expect at the end of it. How fine it is to
enter some old town, walled and turreted, just at
the approach of night-fall, or to come to some strag-
gling village, with the lights streaming through the
surrounding gloom; and then after inquiring for the
best entertainment that the place affords, to "take
one's ease at one's inn." These eventful moments
in our lives' history are too precious, too full of solid
heart-felt happiness to be frittered and dribbled
away in imperfect sympathy. I would have them
all to myself, and drain them to the last drop: they
will do to talk of or to write about afterwards. What
a delicate speculation it is, after drinking whole gob-
lets of tea,—

"The cups that cheer, but not inebriate," —

and letting the fumes ascend into the brain, to sit
considering what we shall have for supper — eggs
and a rasher, a rabbit smothered in onions, or an
excellent veal-cutlet! Sancho in such a situation
once fixed upon cow-heel; and his choice, though he
could not help it, is not to be disparaged. Then in
the intervals of pictured scenery and Shandean contemplation, to catch the preparation and the stir

in the kitchen — *Procul, O procul este profani!*[5]
These hours are sacred to silence and to musing, to
be treasured up in the memory, and to feed the source
of smiling thoughts hereafter. I would not waste
them in idle talk; or if I must have the integrity of
fancy broken in upon, I would rather it were by a
stranger than by a friend. A stranger takes the hue
and character from the time and place; he is a part
of the furniture and costume of an inn. If he is a
Quaker, or from the West Riding of Yorkshire, so
much the better. I do not even try to sympathize
with him, and he breaks no squares. I associate
nothing with my travelling companion but present
objects and passing events. In his ignorance of
me and my affairs, I in a manner forget myself.
But a friend reminds me of other things, rips up old
grievances, and destroys the abstraction of the
scene. He comes in ungraciously between us and
our imaginary character. Something is dropped
in the course of conversation that gives a hint of your
profession and pursuits; or from having some one
with you that knows the less sublime portions
of your history, it seems that other people do. You
are no longer a citizen of the world: but your "un-
housed free condition is put into circumscription and
confine." The *incognito* of an inn is one of its
striking privileges — "lord of one's-self, uncumber'd
with a name." Oh! it is great to shake off the tram-
mels of the world and of public opinion — to lose
our importunate, tormenting, everlasting personal
identity in the elements of nature, and become the
creature of the moment, clear of all ties — to hold
to the universe only by a dish of sweet-breads, and
to owe nothing but the score of the evening — and

no longer seeking for applause and meeting with
contempt, to be known by no other title than *the
Gentleman in the parlour!* One may take one's choice
of all characters in this romantic state of uncertainty
as to one's real pretensions, and become indefinitely
respectable and negatively right-worshipful. We
baffle prejudice and disappoint conjecture; and from
being so to others, begin to be objects of curiosity
and wonder even to ourselves. We are no more
those hackneyed commonplaces that we appear in
the world: an inn restores us to the level of nature
and quits scores with society! I have certainly
spent some enviable hours at inns — sometimes when
I have been left entirely to myself, and have tried to
solve some metaphysical problem, as once at Witham-
common, where I found out the proof that likeness is
not a case of the association of ideas — at other
times, when there have been pictures in the room, as
at St. Neot's (I think it was), where I first met with
Gribelin's engravings [6] of the Cartoons, into which
I entered at once, and at a little inn on the borders
of Wales, where there happened to be hanging some
of Westall's drawings, which I compared triumphantly
(for a theory that I had, not for the admired artist)
with the figure of a girl who had ferried me over the
Severn, standing up in the boat between me and the
twilight — at other times I might mention luxuriat-
ing in books, with a peculiar interest in this way, as
I remember sitting up half the night to read *Paul and
Virginia*,[7] which I picked up at an inn in Bridgewater,
after being drenched in the rain all day; and at the
same place I got through two volumes of Madame
D'Arblay's *Camilla*.[8] It was on the tenth of April,
1798, that I sat down to a volume of the *New Éloïse*,[9]

at the inn at Llangollen, over a bottle of sherry and
a cold chicken. The letter I chose was that in which
St. Preux describes his feelings as he first caught a
glimpse from the heights of the Jura of the Pays de
Vaud, which I had brought with me as a *bon bouche* [10]
to crown the evening with. It was my birthday, and
I had for the first time come from a place in the
neighbourhood to visit this delightful spot. The road
to Llangollen turns off between Chirk and Wrexham;
and on passing a certain point, you come all at once
upon the valley, which opens like an amphitheatre,
broad, barren hills rising in majestic state on either
side, with "green upland swells that echo to the bleat
of flocks" below, and the river Dee babbling over its
stony bed in the midst of them. The valley at this
time "glittered green with sunny showers," and a
budding ash-tree dipped its tender branches in the
chiding stream. How proud, how glad I was to walk
along the high road that overlooks the delicious prospect, repeating the lines which I have just quoted
from Mr. Coleridge's poems! But besides the prospect which opened beneath my feet, another also
opened to my inward sight, a heavenly vision, on
which were written, in letters large as Hope could
make them, these four words, LIBERTY, GENIUS,
LOVE, VIRTUE; which have since faded into the light
of common day, or mock my idle gaze.

"The beautiful is vanished, and returns not."

Still I would return some time or other to this enchanted spot; but I would return to it alone. What
other self could I find to share that influx of thoughts,
of regret, and delight, the fragments of which I could
hardly conjure up to myself, so much have they been

broken and defaced! I could stand on some tall
rock, and overlook the precipice of years that separates me from what I then was. I was at that
time going shortly to visit the poet whom I have above
named. Where is he now? Not only I myself have
changed; the world, which was then new to me, has
become old and incorrigible. Yet will I turn to thee
in thought, O sylvan Dee, in joy, in youth and glad-
ness as thou then wert; and thou shalt always be to
me the river of Paradise, where I will drink of the
waters of life freely!

There is hardly any thing that shows the short-
sightedness or capriciousness of the imagination
more than travelling does. With change of place
we change our ideas; nay, our opinions and feelings.
We can by an effort indeed transport ourselves to old
and long-forgotten scenes, and then the picture of
the mind revives again; but we forget those that we
have just left. It seems that we can think of but
one place at a time. The canvas of the fancy is but
of a certain extent, and if we paint one set of objects
upon it, they immediately efface every other. We
cannot enlarge our conceptions, we only shift our
point of view. The landscape bares its bosom to the
enraptured eye, we take our fill of it, and seem as if
we could form no other image of beauty or grandeur.
We pass on, and think no more of it: the horizon that
shuts it from our sight, also blots it from our memory
like a dream. In travelling through a wild barren
country, I can form no idea of a woody and cultivated
one. It appears to me that all the world must be barren, like what I see of it. In the country we forget the town, and in town we despise the country.
"Beyond Hyde Park," says Sir Fopling Flutter, "all

Is a desert." All that part of the map that we do not see before us is a blank. The world in our conceit of it is not much bigger than a nutshell. It is not one prospect expanded into another, county joined to county, kingdom to kingdom, lands to seas, making an image voluminous and vast; — the mind can form no larger idea of space than the eye can take in at a single glance. The rest is a name written in a map, a calculation of arithmetic. For instance, what is the true signification of that immense mass of territory and population known by the name of China to us? An inch of paste-board on a wooden globe, of no more account than a China orange! Things near us are seen of the size of life: things at a distance are diminished to the size of the understanding. We measure the universe by ourselves, and even comprehend the texture of our own being only piecemeal. In this way, however, we remember an infinity of things and places. The mind is like a mechanical instrument that plays a great variety of tunes, but it must play them in succession. One idea recalls another, but it at the same time excludes all others. In trying to renew old recollections, we cannot as it were unfold the whole web of our existence; we must pick out the single threads. So in coming to a place where we have formerly lived and with which we have intimate associations, every one must have found that the feeling grows more vivid the nearer we approach the spot, from the mere anticipation of the actual impression: we remember circumstances, feelings, persons, faces, names, that we had not thought of for years; but for the time all the rest of the world is forgotten! — To return to the question I have quitted above.

I have no objection to go to see ruins, aqueducts, pictures, in company with a friend or party, but rather the contrary, for the former reason reversed. They are intelligible matters, and will bear talking about. The sentiment here is not tacit, but communicable and overt. Salisbury Plain is barren of criticism, but Stonehenge [11] will bear a discussion antiquarian, picturesque, and philosophical. In setting out on a party of pleasure, the first consideration always is where shall we go to: in taking a solitary ramble, the question is what shall we meet with by the way. "The mind is its own place;" nor are we anxious to arrive at the end of our journey. I can myself do the honours indifferently well to works of art and curiosity. I once took a party to Oxford with no mean *éclat* — shewed them that seat of the Muses at a distance,—

"With glistering spires and pinnacles adorn'd" —

descanted on the learned air that breathes from the grassy quadrangles and stone walls of halls and colleges — was at home in the Bodleian; [12] and at Blenheim [13] quite superseded the powdered Ciceroni that attended us, and that pointed in vain with his wand to commonplace beauties in matchless pictures. As another exception to the above reasoning, I should not feel confident in venturing on a journey in a foreign country without a companion. I should want at intervals to hear the sound of my own language. There is an involuntary antipathy in the mind of an Englishman to foreign manners and notions that requires the assistance of social sympathy to carry it off. As the distance from home increases, this relief, which was at first a luxury, becomes a passion and an appetite. A person would almost feel stifled to find himself in the deserts of Arabia without friends and countrymen: there must be allowed to be something in the view of Athens or old Rome that claims the utterance of speech; and I own that the Pyramids are too mighty for any single contemplation. In such situations, so opposite to all one's ordinary train of ideas, one seems a species by one's self, a limb torn off from society, unless one can meet with instant fellowship and support. — Yet I did not feel this want or craving very pressing once, when I first set my foot on the laughing shores of France. Calais was peopled with novelty and delight. The confused, busy murmur of the place was like oil and wine poured into my ears; nor did the mariners' hymn, which was sung from the top of an old crazy vessel in the harbour, as the sun went down, send an alien sound into my soul. I only breathed the air of general humanity. I walked over "the vine-covered hills and gay regions of France," erect and satisfied; for the image of man was not cast down and chained to the foot of arbitrary thrones: I was at no loss for language, — for that of all the great schools of painting was open to me. The whole is vanished like a shade. Pictures, heroes, glory, freedom, all are fled: nothing remains but the Bourbons and the French people! — There is undoubtedly a sensation in travelling into foreign parts that is to be had nowhere else: but it is more pleasing at the time than lasting. It is too remote from our habitual associations to be a common topic of discourse or reference, and, like a dream or another state of existence, does not piece into our daily modes of life. It is an animated but a momentary hallucination.

It demands an effort to exchange our actual for our ideal identity, and to feel the pulse of our old transports revive very keenly, we must "jump" all our present comforts and connections. Our romantic and itinerant character is not to be domesticated. Dr. Johnson remarked how little foreign travel added to the facilities of conversation in those who had been abroad. In fact, the time we have spent there is both delightful and in one sense instructive; but it appears to be cut out of our substantial, downright existence, and never to join kindly on to it. We are not the same, but another, and perhaps more enviable individual, all the time we are out of our own country. We are lost to ourselves, as well as our friends. So the poet somewhat quaintly sings,—

"Out of my country and myself I go."

Those who wish to forget painful thoughts, do well to absent themselves for a while from the ties and objects that recall them: but we can be said only to fulfil our destiny in the place that gave us birth. I should on this account like well enough to spend the whole of my life in travelling abroad, if I could anywhere borrow another life to spend afterwards at home! —

ON A SUN-DIAL

"To carve out dials quaintly, point by point."
SHAKESPEARE.

Horas non numero nisi serenas — is the motto of a sun-dial near Venice. There is a softness and a harmony in the words and in the thought unparalleled. Of all conceits it is surely the most classical. "I

count only the hours that are serene." What a
bland and care-dispelling feeling! How the shadows
seem to fade on the dial-plate as the sky lours, and
time presents only a blank unless as its progress is
marked by what is joyous, and all that is not happy
sinks into oblivion! What a fine lesson is conveyed
to the mind — to take no note of time but by its
benefits, to watch only for the smiles and neglect
the frowns of fate, to compose our lives of bright and
gentle moments, turning always to the sunny side
of things, and letting the rest slip from our imaginations, unheeded or forgotten! How different
from the common art of self-tormenting! For myself, as I rode along the Brenta, while the sun shone
hot upon its sluggish, slimy waves, my sensations
were far from comfortable; but the reading this in-
scription on the side of a glaring wall in an instant
restored me to myself; and still, whenever I think
of or repeat it, it has the power of wafting me into
the region of pure and blissful abstraction. I cannot
help fancying it to be a legend of Popish superstition.
Some monk of the dark ages must have invented and
bequeathed it to us, who, loitering in trim gardens
and watching the silent march of time, as his fruits
ripened in the sun or his flowers scented the balmy
air, felt a mild languor pervade his senses, and having
little to do or to care for, determined (in imitation of
his sun-dial) to efface that little from his thoughts or
draw a veil over it, making of his life one long dream
of quiet. *Horas non numero nisi serenas* — he
might repeat, when the heavens were overcast, and
the gathering storm scattered the falling leaves, and
turn to his books and wrap himself in his golden
studies! Out of some such mood of mind, indolent

elegant, thoughtful, this exquisite device (speaking volumes) must have originated.

Of the several modes of counting time, that by the sun-dial is perhaps the most apposite and striking, if not the most convenient or comprehensive. It does not obtrude its observations, though it "morals on the time," and, by its stationary character, forms a contrast to the most fleeting of all essences. It stands *sub dio* — under the marble air, and there is some connexion between the image of infinity and eternity. I should also like to have a sun-flower growing near it with bees fluttering round. It should be of iron to denote duration, and have a dull, leaden look. I hate a sun-dial made of wood, which is rather calculated to show the variations of the seasons, than the progress of time, slow, silent, imperceptible, chequered with light and shade. If our hours were all serene, we might probably take almost as little note of them as the dial does of those that are clouded. It is the shadow thrown across, that gives us warning of their flight. Otherwise our impressions would take the same undistinguishable hue; we should scarce be conscious of our existence. Those who have had none of the cares of this life to harass and disturb them, have been obliged to have recourse to the hopes and fears of the next to vary the prospect before them. Most of the methods for measuring the lapse of time have, I believe, been the contrivance of monks and religious recluses, who, finding time hang heavy on their hands, were at some pains to see how they got rid of it. The hour-glass is, I suspect, an older invention; and it is certainly the most defective of all. Its creeping sands are not indeed an unapt emblem of the minute, countless portions of our existence; and the manner in which they gradually slide through the hollow glass and diminish in number till not a single one is left, also illustrates the way in which our years slip from us by stealth: but as a mechanical invention, it is rather a hindrance than a help, for it requires to have the time, of which it pretends to count the precious moments, taken up in attention to itself, and in seeing that when one end of the glass is empty, we turn it round, in order that it may go on again, or else all our labour is lost, and we must wait for some other mode of ascertaining the time before we can recover our reckoning and proceed as before. The philosopher in his cell, the cottager at her spinning-wheel must, however, find an invaluable acquisition in this "companion of the lonely hour," as it has been called, which not only serves to tell how the time goes, but to fill up its vacancies. What a treasure must not the little box seem to hold, as if it were a sacred deposit of the very grains and fleeting sands of life! What a business, in lieu of other more important avocations, to see it out to the last sand, and then to renew the process again on the instant, that there may not be the least flaw or error in the account! What a strong sense must be brought home to the mind of the value and irrecoverable nature of the time that is fled; what a thrilling incessant consciousness of the slippery tenure by which we hold what remains of it! Our very existence must seem crumbling to atoms, and running down (without a miraculous reprieve) to the last fragment. "Dust to dust and ashes to ashes" is a text that might be fairly inscribed on an hour-glass: it is ordinarily associated with the scythe of Time and a Death's-head, as a *memento mori;*[1]

and has, no doubt, furnished many a tacit hint to the apprehensive and visionary enthusiast in favour of a resurrection to another life!

The French give a different turn to things, less *sombre* and less edifying. A common and also a very pleasing ornament to a clock, in Paris, is a figure of Time seated in a boat which Cupid is rowing along, with the motto, *L'Amour fait passer le Temps* — which the wits again have travestied into *Le Temps fait passer L'Amour*.[2] All this is ingenious and well; but it wants sentiment. I like a people who have something that they love and something that they hate, and with whom everything is not alike a matter of indifference or *pour passer le temps*. The French attach no importance to anything, except for the moment; they are only thinking how they shall get rid of one sensation for another; all their ideas are *in transitu*.[3] Everything is detached, nothing is accumulated. It would be a million of years before a Frenchman would think of the *Horas non numero nisi serenas*. Its impassioned repose and *ideal* voluptuousness are as far from their breasts as the poetry of that line in Shakespeare — "How sweet the moonlight sleeps upon this bank!" They never arrive at the classical — or the romantic. They blow the bubbles of vanity, fashion, and pleasure; but they do not expand their perceptions into refinement, or strengthen them into solidity. Where there is nothing fine in the groundwork of the imagination, nothing fine in the superstructure can be produced. They are light, airy, fanciful (to give them their due) — but when they attempt to be serious (beyond mere good sense) they are either dull or extravagant. When the volatile salt has flown off, nothing but a

caput mortuum[4] remains. They have infinite crotch-
ets and caprices with their clocks and watches,
which seem made for anything but to tell the hour —
gold repeaters, watches with metal covers, clocks
with hands to count the seconds. There is no escaping from quackery and impertinence, even in our
attempts to calculate the waste of time. The years
gallop fast enough for me, without remarking every
moment as it flies; and further, I must say I dislike
a watch (whether of French or English manufacture),
that comes to me like a footpad with its face muffled,
and does not present its clear, open aspect like a friend,
and point with its finger to the time of day. All this
opening and shutting of dull, heavy cases (under pretence that the glass-lid is liable to be broken, or lets in
the dust or air and obstructs the movements of the
watch), is not to husband time, but to give trouble.
It is mere pomposity and self-importance, like con-
sulting a mysterious oracle that one carries about with
one in one's pocket, instead of asking a common
question of an acquaintance or companion. There are
two clocks which strike the hour in the room where I
am. This I do not like. In the first place, I do not
want to be reminded twice how the time goes (it
is like the second tap of a saucy servant at your door
when perhaps you have no wish to get up): in the
next place, it is starting a difference of opinion on the
subject, and I am averse to every appearance of
wrangling and disputation. Time moves on the same,
whatever disparity there may be in our mode of keeping count of it, like true fame in spite of the cavils
and contradictions of the critics. I am no friend to
repeating watches. The only pleasant association
I have with them is the account given by Rousseau

of some French lady, who sat up reading the *New
Éloïse* when it first came out, and ordering her maid
to sound the repeater, found it was too late to go to
bed, and continued reading on until morning. Yet
how different is the interest excited by this story
from the account which Rousseau somewhere else
gives of his sitting up with his father reading romances,
when a boy, till they were startled by the swallows
twittering in their nests at daybreak, and the father
cried out, half angry and ashamed — "*Allons, mon
fils; je suis plus enfant que toi!*" [5] In general, I have
heard repeating watches sounded in stage-coaches
at night, when some fellow-traveller suddenly awak-
ing and wondering what was the hour, another has
deliberately taken out his watch, and pressing the
spring, it has counted out the time; each petty
stroke acting like a sharp puncture on the ear, and
informing me of the dreary hours I had already
passed, and of the more dreary ones I had to wait till
morning.

The great advantage, it is true, which clocks have
over watches and other dumb reckoners of time is,
that for the most part they strike the hour — that
they are as it were the mouthpieces of time; that
they not only point it to the eye, but impress it on
the ear; that they "lend it both an understanding
and a tongue." Time thus speaks to us in an audible
and warning voice. Objects of sight are easily distinguished by the sense, and suggest useful reflections
to the mind; sounds, from their intermittent nature,
and perhaps other causes, appeal more to the imagination, and strike upon the heart. But to do this,
they must be unexpected and voluntary — there must
be no trick in the case — they should not be squeezed

out with a finger and thumb; there should be nothing optional, personal in their occurrence; they should be like stern, inflexible monitors, that nothing can prevent from discharging their duty. Surely, if there is anything with which we should not mix up our vanity and self-consequence, it is with Time, the most independent of all things. All the sublimity, all the superstition that hang upon this palpable mode of announcing its flight, are chiefly attached to this circumstance. Time would lose its abstracted character, if we kept it like a curiosity or a jack-in-a-box: its prophetic warnings would have no effect, if it obviously spoke only at our prompting like a paltry ventriloquism. The clock that tells the coming, dreaded hour — the castle bell, that "with its brazen throat and iron tongue, sounds *one* unto the drowsy ear of night"— the curfew, "swinging slow with sullen roar" o'er wizard stream or fountain, are like a voice from other worlds, big with unknown events. The last sound, which is still kept up as an old custom in many parts of England, is a great favourite with me. I used to hear it when a boy. It tells a tale of other times. The days that are past, the generations that are gone, the tangled forest glades and hamlets brown of my native country, the woodsman's art, the Norman warrior armed for the battle or in his festive hall, the conqueror's iron rule and peasant's lamp extinguished, all start up at the clamorous peal, and fill my mind with fear and wonder. I confess, nothing at present interests me but what has been — the recollection of the impressions of my early life, or events long past, of which only the dim traces remain in a mouldering ruin or half-obsolete custom. That *things should be*

that are now no more, creates in my mind the most
unfeigned astonishment. I cannot solve the mystery
of the past, nor exhaust my pleasure in it. The years,
the generations to come, are nothing to me. We care
no more about the world in the year 2300 than
we do about one of the planets. We might as well
make a voyage to the moon as think of stealing upon
Time with impunity. *De non apparentibus et non
existentibus eadem est ratio.*[6] Those who are to come
after us and push us from the stage seem like up-
starts and pretenders, that may be said to exist *in
vacuo,*[7] we know not upon what, except as they are
blown up with vanity and self-conceit by their
patrons among the moderns. But the ancients are
true and *bona fide* people, to whom we are bound by
aggregate knowledge and filial ties, and in whom,
seen by the mellow light of history, we feel our own
existence doubled and our pride consoled, as we
ruminate on the vestiges of the past. The public in
general, however, do not carry this speculative indifference about the future to what is to happen to
themselves, or to the part they are to act in the busy
scene. For my own part, I do; and the only wish I
can form, or that ever prompts the passing sign, would
be to live some of my years over again — they would
be those in which I enjoyed and suffered most!

The ticking of a clock in the night has nothing very
interesting nor very alarming about it, though superstition has magnified it into an omen. In a state
of vigilance or debility, it preys upon the spirits like
the persecution of a teazing, pertinacious insect;
and haunting the imagination after it has ceased in
reality, is converted into the death-watch. Time is
rendered vast by contemplating its minute portions

thus repeatedly and painfully urged upon its attention, as the ocean in its immensity is composed of water-drops. A clock striking with a clear and silver sound is a great relief in such circumstances, breaks the spell, and resembles a sylph-like and friendly spirit in the room. Foreigners with all their tricks and contrivances upon clocks and time-pieces, are strangers to the sound of village-bells, though perhaps a people that can dance may dispense with them. They impart a pensive, wayward pleasure to the mind, and are a kind of chronology of happy events, often serious in the retrospect — births, marriages, and so forth. Coleridge calls them "the poor man's only music." A village-spire in England peeping from its cluster of trees, is always associated in imagination with this cheerful accompaniment, and may be expected to pour its joyous tidings on the gale. In Catholic countries, you are stunned with the everlasting tolling of bells to prayers or for the dead. In the Apennines, and other wild and mountainous districts of Italy, the little chapel-bell with its simple tinkling sound has a romantic and charming effect. The monks in former times appear to have taken a pride in the construction of bells as well as churches; and some of those of the great cathedrals abroad (as at Cologne and Rouen) may be fairly said to be hoarse with counting the flight of ages. The chimes in Holland are a nuisance. They dance in the hours and the quarters. They leave no respite to the imagination. Before one set has done ringing in your ears, another begins. You do not know whether the hours move or stand still, go backwards or forwards, so fantastical and perplexing are their accompaniments. Time is a more staid personage, and not so full of gambols. It puts you in mind of a tune with variations, or of an embroidered dress. Surely, nothing is more simple than time. His march is straightforward; but we should have leisure allowed us to look back upon the distance we have come, and not be counting his steps every moment. Time in Holland is a foolish old fellow with all the antics of a youth, who "goes to church in a coranto, and lights his pipe in a cinque-pace." The chimes with us, on the contrary, as they come in every three or four hours, are like stages in the journey of the day. They give a fillip to the lazy, creeping hours, and relieve the lassitude of country-places. At noon, their desultory, trivial song is diffused through the hamlet with the odour of rashers of bacon; at the close of day they send the toil-worn sleepers to their beds. Their discontinuance would be a great loss to the thinking or unthinking public. Mr. Wordsworth has painted their effect on the mind when he makes his friend Matthew, in a fit of inspired dotage,

> "Sing those witty rhymes
> About the crazy old church-clock
> And the bewilder'd chimes."

The tolling of the bell for deaths and executions is a fearful summons, though, as it announces, not the advance of time but the approach of fate, it happily makes no part of our subject. Otherwise, the "sound of the bell" for Macheath's execution in the *Beggar's Opera*,[8] or for that of the Conspirators in *Venice Preserved*,[9] with the roll of the drum at a soldier's funeral, and a digression to that of my uncle Toby, as it is so finely described by Sterne, would furnish ample topics to descant upon. If

I were a moralist, I might disapprove the ringing in
the new and ringing out the old year.

"Why dance ye, mortals, o'er the grave of Time?"

St. Paul's bell tolls only for the death of our English
kings, or a distinguished personage or two, with long
intervals between.

Those who have no artificial means of ascertaining
the progress of time are in general the most acute
in discerning its immediate signs, and are most reten-
tive of individual dates. The mechanical aids to
knowledge are not sharpeners of wits. The understanding of a savage is a kind of natural almanac,
and more true in its prognostication of the future.
In his mind's eye he sees what has happened or what
is likely to happen to him, "as in a map the voyager
his course." Those who read the times and seasons in
the aspect of the heavens and the configuration of the
stars, who count by moons and know when the sun
rises and sets, are by no means ignorant of their
own affairs or of the common concatenation of events.
People in such situations have not their faculties dis-
tracted by any multiplicity of inquiries beyond what
befalls themselves, and the outward appearances that
mark the change. There is, therefore, a simplicity
and clearness in the knowledge they possess, which
often puzzles the more learned. I am sometimes surprised at a shepherd boy by the roadside, who sees
nothing but the earth and sky, asking me the time
of day — he ought to know so much better than any-
one how far the sun is above the horizon. I suppose
he wants to ask a question of a passenger, or to see
if he has a watch. Robinson Crusoe lost his reckoning in the monotony of his life and that bewildering

dream of solitude, and was fain to have recourse to the notches in a piece of wood. What a diary was his! And how time must have spread its circuit round him, vast and pathless as the ocean!

For myself, I have never had a watch nor any other mode of keeping time in my possession, nor ever wish to learn how time goes. It is a sign I have had little to do, few avocations, few engagements. When I am in a town, I can hear the clock; and when I am in the country, I can listen to the silence. What I like best is to lie whole mornings on a sunny bank on Salisbury Plain, without any object before me, neither knowing nor caring how time passes, and thus "with light-winged toys of feathered Idleness" to melt down hours to moments. Perhaps some such thoughts as I have here set down float before me like motes before my half-shut eyes, or some vivid image of the past by forcible contrast rushes by me— "Diana and her fawn, and all the glories of the an- tique world;" then I start away to prevent the iron from entering my soul, and let fall some tears into that hot stream of time which separates me farther and farther from all I once loved! At length I rouse myself from my reverie, and home to dinner, proud of killing time with thought, nay even without think- ing. Somewhat of this idle humour I inherit from my father, though he had not the same freedom from *ennui*, for he was not a metaphysician; and there were stops and vacant intervals in his being which he did not know how to fill up. He used in these cases, and as an obvious resource, carefully to wind up his watch at night, and "with lack-lustre eye" more than once in the course of the day look to see what o'clock it was. Yet he had nothing else in his char-

acter in common with the elder Mr. Shandy. Were I
to attempt a sketch of him, for my own or the reader's
satisfaction, it would be after the following manner
——— But now I recollect I have done something of
the kind once before, and were I to resume the subject here, some bat or owl of a critic, with specta-
cled gravity, might swear I had stolen the whole of
this Essay from myself — or (what is worse) from him!
So I had better let it go as it is.

ON THE FEELING OF IMMORTALITY IN YOUTH

No young man believes he shall ever die. It was
a saying of my brother's, and a fine one. There is
a feeling of Eternity in youth which makes amends
for everything. To be young is to be as one of the
Immortals. One half of time, indeed, is spent — the
other half remains in store for us with all its countless treasures, for there is no line drawn, and we
see no limit to our hopes and wishes. We make the
coming age our own —

> "The vast, the unbounded prospect lies before us."

Death, old age, are words without a meaning, a dream,
a fiction, with which we have nothing to do. Others
may have undergone, or may still undergo them —
we "bear a charmed life," which laughs to scorn all
such idle fancies. As, in setting out on a delightful
journey, we strain our eager sight forward,—

> "Bidding the lovely scenes at distance hail," —

and see no end to prospect after prospect, new objects
presenting themselves as we advance, so in the out-

set of life we see no end to our desires nor to the opportunities of gratifying them. We have as yet found
no obstacle, no disposition to flag, and it seems that
we can go on so forever. We look round in a new
world, full of life and motion, and ceaseless progress,
and feel in ourselves all the vigour and spirit to keep
pace with it, and do not foresee from any present
signs how we shall be left behind in the race, decline
into old age, and drop into the grave. It is the simplicity, and, as it were, abstractedness of our feelings
in youth that (so to speak) identifies us with nature
and (our experience being weak and our passions
strong) makes us fancy ourselves immortal like it.
Our short-lived connection with being, we fondly
flatter ourselves, is an indissoluble and lasting union.
As infants smile and sleep, we are rocked in the
cradle of our desires, and hushed into fancied security
by the roar of the universe around us — we quaff the
cup of life with eager thirst without draining it, and
joy and hope seem ever mantling to the brim—objects
press around us, filling the mind with their magnitude
and with the throng of desires that wait upon them,
so that there is no room for the thoughts of death.
We are too much dazzled by the gorgeousness and
novelty of the bright waking dream about us to
discern the dim shadow lingering for us in the distance. Nor would the hold that life has taken of
us permit us to detach our thoughts that way, even
if we could. We are too much absorbed in present
objects and pursuits. While the spirit of youth
remains unimpaired, ere "the wine of life is drunk,"
we are like people intoxicated or in a fever, who are
hurried away by the violence of their own sensations:
it is only as present objects begin to pall upon the

sense, as we have been disappointed in our favourite pursuits, cut off from our closest ties, that we by degrees become weaned from the world, that passion loosens its hold upon futurity, and that we begin to contemplate as in a glass darkly the possibility of parting with it for good. Till then, the example of others has no effect upon us. Casualities we avoid; the slow approaches of age we play at *hide and seek* with. Like the foolish fat scullion in Sterne, who hears that Master Bobby is dead, our only reflection is, "So am not I!" The idea of death, instead of staggering our confidence, only seems to strengthen and enhance our sense of the possession and enjoyment of life. Others may fall around us like leaves, or be mowed down by the scythe of Time like grass: these are but metaphors to the unreflecting, buoyant ears and overweening presumption of youth. It is not till we see the flowers of Love, Hope, and Joy withering around us, that we give up the flattering delusions that before led us on, and that the emptiness and dreariness of the prospect before us reconciles us hypothetically to the silence of the grave.

Life is indeed a strange gift, and its privileges are most mysterious. No wonder when it is first granted to us, that our gratitude, our admiration, and our delight should prevent us from reflecting on our own nothingness, or from thinking it will ever be recalled. Our first and strongest impressions are borrowed from the mighty scene that is open to us, and we unconsciously transfer its durability as well as its splendour to ourselves. So newly found, we cannot think of parting with it yet, or at least put off that consideration *sine die*. Like a rustic at a fair, we are full of amazement and rapture, and have no thought of going home, or that it will soon be night. We know our existence only by ourselves, and confound our knowledge with the objects of it. We and Nature are therefore one. Otherwise the illusion, the "feast of reason and the flow of soul," to which we are invited, is a mockery and a cruel insult. We do not go from a play till the last act is ended, and the lights are about to be extinguished. But the fairy face of Nature still shines on: shall we be called away before the curtain falls, or ere we have scarce had a glimpse of what is going on? Like children, our stepmother Nature holds us up to see the raree-show of the universe, and then, as if we were a burden to her to support, lets us fall down again. Yet what brave sublunary things does not this pageant present, like a ball or *fête* of the universe!

To see the golden sun, the azure sky, the outstretched ocean; to walk upon the green earth, and be lord of a thousand creatures; to look down yawning precipices or over distant sunny vales; to see the world spread out under one's feet on a map; to bring the stars near; to view the smallest insects through a microscope; to read history, and consider the revolutions of empire and the successions of generations; to hear of the glory of Tyre, of Sidon, of Babylon, and of Susa, and to say all these were before me and are now nothing; to say I exist in such a point of time, and in such a point of space; to be a spectator and a part of its ever-moving scene; to witness the change of season, of spring and autumn, of winter and summer; to feel hot and cold, pleasure and pain, beauty and deformity, right and wrong; to be sensible to the accidents of Nature; to consider the mighty world of eye

and ear; to listen to the stock-dove's notes amid the
forest deep; to journey over moor and mountain;
to hear the midnight sainted choir; to visit lighted
halls, or the cathedral's gloom, or sit in crowded
theatres and see life itself mocked; to study the works
of art and refine the sense of beauty to agony; to
worship fame, and to dream of immortality; to look
upon the Vatican, and to read Shakespeare; to gather
up the wisdom of the ancients, and to pry into the
future; to listen to the trump of war, the shout
of victory; to question history as to the movements of
the human heart; to seek for truth; to plead the
cause of humanity; to overlook the world as if time
and nature poured their treasures at our feet —
to be and to do all this, and then in a moment to
be nothing — to have it all snatched from us as by
a juggler's trick, or a phantasmagoria! There is something in this transition from all to nothing that shocks
us and damps the enthusiasm of youth new flushed
with hope and pleasure, and we cast the comfortless
thought as far from us as we can. In the first enjoyment of the estate of life we discard the fear of debts
and duns, and never think of the final payment of our
great debt to Nature. Art we know is long; life, we
flatter ourselves, should be so too. We see no end of
the difficulties and delays we have to encounter;
perfection is slow of attainment, and we must have
time to accomplish it in. The fame of the great names
we look up to is immortal; and shall not we who contemplate it imbibe a portion of ethereal fire, the *divinæ particula auræ*,[1] which nothing can extinguish?
A wrinkle in Rembrandt or in Nature takes whole days
to resolve itself into its component parts, its softenings
and its sharpnesses; we refine upon our perfections, and

unfold the intricacies of nature. What a prospect for
the future! What a task have we not begun! And
shall we be arrested in the middle of it? We do not
count our time thus employed lost, or our pains thrown
away; we do not flag or grow tired, but gain new vigour at our endless task. Shall Time, then, grudge
us to finish what we have begun, and have formed
a compact with Nature to do? Why not fill up the
blank that is left us in this manner? I have looked for
hours at a Rembrandt without being conscious of the
flight of time, but with ever new wonder and delight, have thought that not only my own but another
existence I could pass in the same manner. This rare-
fied, refined existence seemed to have no end, nor
stint, nor principle of decay in it. The print would
remain long after I who looked on it had become the
prey of worms. The thing seems in itself out of all
reason; health, strength, appetite are opposed to the
idea of death, and we are not ready to credit it till
we have found our illusions vanished, and our hopes
grown cold. Objects in youth, from novelty, &c., are
stamped upon the brain with such force and integrity
that one thinks nothing can remove or obliterate them.
They are riveted there, and appear to us as an element
of our nature. It must be a mere violence that
destroys them, not a natural decay. In the very
strength of this persuasion we seem to enjoy an age
by anticipation. We melt down years into a single
moment of intense sympathy, and by anticipating
the fruits defy the ravages of time. If, then, a single
moment of our lives is worth years, shall we set any
limits to its total value and extent? Again, does
it not happen that so secure do we think ourselves
of an indefinite period of existence, that at times

when left to ourselves, and impatient of novelty, we feel annoyed at what seems to us the slow and creeping progress of time, and argue that if it always moves at this tedious snail's pace it will never come to an end? How ready are we to sacrifice any space of time that separates us from a favourite object, little thinking that before long we shall find it too fast.

For my own part, I started in life with the French Revolution, and I have lived, alas! to see the end of it. But I did not foresee this result. My sun arose with the first dawn of liberty, and I did not think how soon both must set. The new impulse to ardour given to men's minds imparted a congenial warmth and glow to mine; we were strong to run a race together, and I little dreamed that long before mine was set, the sun of liberty would turn to blood, or set once more in the night of despotism. Since then, I confess, I have no longer felt myself young, for with that my hopes fell.

I have since turned my thoughts to gathering up some of the fragments of my early recollections, and putting them into a form to which I might occasionally revert. The future was barred to my progress, and I turned for consolation and encouragement to the past. It is thus that, while we find our personal and substantial identity vanishing from us, we strive to gain a reflected and vicarious one in our thoughts: we do not like to perish wholly, and wish to bequeath our names, at least, to posterity. As long as we can make our cherished thoughts and nearest interests live in the minds of others, we do not appear to have retired altogether from the stage. We still occupy the breasts of others, and exert an influence and power over them. and it is only our bodies that

are reduced to dust and powder. Our favourite specu-
lations still find encouragement, and we make as
great a figure in the eye of the world, or perhaps a
greater, than in our lifetime. The demands of our
self-love are thus satisfied, and these are the most
imperious and unremitting. Besides, if by our intellectual superiority we survive ourselves in this world,
by our virtues and faith we may attain an interest
in another, and a higher state of being, and may thus
be recipients at the same time of men and angels.

"E'en from the tomb the voice of Nature cries,
  E'en in our ashes live their wonted fires."

As we grow old, our sense of the value of time becomes
vivid. Nothing else, indeed, seems of any consequence.
We can never cease wondering that that which has
ever been should cease to be. We find many things
remain the same: why then should there be change
in us? This adds a convulsive grasp of whatever is,
a sense of a fallacious hollowness in all we see. Instead of the full, pulpy feeling of youth tasting existence and every object in it, all is flat and vapid,
— a whited sepulchre, fair without but full of raven-
ing and all uncleanness within. The world is a witch
that puts us off with false shows and appearances.
The simplicity of youth, the confiding expectation,
the boundless raptures, are gone: we only think of
getting out of it as well as we can, and without any
great mischance or annoyance. The flush of illusion,
even the complacent retrospect of past joys and hopes,
is over: if we can slip out of life without indignity, can
escape with little bodily infirmity, and frame our
minds to the calm and respectable composure of
still-life before we return to physical nothingness,

it is as much as we can expect. We do not die wholly at our deaths: we have mouldered away gradually long before. Faculty after faculty, interest after interest, attachment after attachment disappear: we are torn from ourselves while living, year after year sees us no longer the same, and death only consigns the last fragment of what we were to the grave. That we should wear out by slow stages, and dwindle at last into nothing, is not wonderful, when even in our prime our strongest impressions leave little trace but for the moment, and we are the creatures of petty circumstance. How little effect is made on us in our best days by the books we have read, the scenes we have witnessed, the sensations we have gone through! Think only of the feelings we experience in reading a fine romance (one of Sir Walter's, for instance); what beauty, what sublimity, what interest, what heart-rending emotions! You would suppose the feelings you then experienced would last for ever, or subdue the mind to their own harmony and tone: while we are reading it seems as if nothing could ever put us out of our way, or trouble us: — the first splash of mud that we get on entering the street, the first twopence we are cheated out of, the feeling vanishes clean out of our minds, and we become the prey of petty and annoying circumstance. The mind soars to the lofty: it is at home in the grovelling, the disagreeable, and the little. And yet we wonder that age should be so feeble and querulous, — that the freshness of youth should fade away. Both worlds would hardly satisfy the extravagance of our desires and of our presumption.

THOMAS DE QUINCEY

THE VISION OF SUDDEN DEATH

WHAT is to be taken as the predominant opinion
of man, reflective and philosophic, upon SUDDEN
DEATH? It is remarkable that, in different conditions of society, sudden death has been variously
regarded as the consummation of an earthly career
most fervently to be desired, or, again, as that consummation which is with most horror to be deprecated.
Cæsar, the Dictator, at his last dinner party (*cæna*),
on the very evening before his assassination, when the
minutes of his earthly career were numbered, being
asked what death, in *his* judgment, might be pronounced the most eligible, replied, "That which
should be most sudden." On the other hand, the
divine Litany of our English Church, when breathing
forth supplications as if in some representative character for the whole human race prostrate before God,
places such a death in the very van of horrors:
"From lightning and tempest; from plague, pesti-
lence, and famine; from battle and murder, and from
SUDDEN DEATH — *Good Lord, deliver us.*" Sudden
death is here made to crown the climax in a grand
ascent of calamities; it is ranked among the last of
curses; and yet, by the noblest of Romans, it was
ranked as the first of blessings. In that difference
most readers will see little more than the essential
difference between Christianity and Paganism. But
this, on consideration, I doubt. The Christian

Church may be right in its estimate of sudden death; and it is a natural feeling, though after all it may also be an infirm one, to wish for a quiet dismissal from life — as that which *seems* most reconcilable with meditation, with penitential retrospects, and with the humilities of farewell prayer. There does not, however, occur to me any direct scriptural warrant for this earnest petition of the English Litany, unless under a special construction of the word "sudden." It seems a petition indulged, rather, and conceded to human infirmity, than exacted from human piety. It is not so much a doctrine built upon the eternities of the Christian system, as a plausible opinion built upon special varieties of physical temperament. Let that, however, be as it may, two remarks suggest themselves as prudent restraints upon a doctrine which else *may* wander, and *has* wandered, into an uncharitable superstition. The first is this: that many people are likely to exaggerate the horror of a sudden death from the disposition to lay a false stress upon words or acts simply because by an accident they have become *final* words or acts. If a man dies, for instance, by some sudden death when he happens to be intoxicated, such a death is falsely regarded with peculiar horror; as though the intoxication were suddenly exalted into a blasphemy. But *that* is unphilosophic. The man was, or he was not, *habitually* a drunkard. If not, if this intoxication were a solitary accident, there can be no reason for allowing special emphasis to this act simply because through misfortune it became his final act. Nor, on the other hand, if it were no accident, but one of his *habitual* transgressions, will it be the more habitual or the more a transgression because some sudden calamity,

surprising him, has caused this habitual transgression
to be also a final one. Could the man have had any
reason even dimly to foresee his own sudden death,
there would have been a new feature in his act of
intemperance — a feature of presumption and irrev-
erence, as in one that, having known himself drawing near to the presence of God, should have suited
his demeanour to an expectation so awful. But this
is no part of the case supposed. And the only new element in the man's act is not any element of special
immorality, but simply of special misfortune.

The other remark has reference to the meaning of
the word *sudden*. Very possibly Cæsar and the
Christian Church do not differ in the way supposed,
— that is, do not differ by any difference of doctrine
as between Pagan and Christian views of the moral
temper appropriate to death; but perhaps they are
contemplating different cases. Both contemplate a
violent death, a βιαθανατος — death that is βιαιος,
or, in other words, death that is brought about, not
by internal and spontaneous change, but by active
force having its origin from without. In this meaning the two authorities agree. Thus far they are in
harmony. But the difference is that the Roman by
the word "sudden" means *unlingering*, whereas the
Christian Litany by "sudden death" means a death
without warning, consequently without any available
summons to religious preparation. The poor mutineer
who kneels down to gather into his heart the bullets
from twelve firelocks of his pitying comrades dies
by a most sudden death in Cæsar's sense; one shock,
one mighty spasm, one (possibly *not* one) groan, and
all is over. But, in the sense of the Litany, the mutineer's death is far from sudden: his offence originally,

his imprisonment, his trial, the interval between his sentence and its execution, having all furnished him with separate warnings of his fate — having all summoned him to meet it with solemn preparation.

Here at once, in this sharp verbal distinction, we comprehend the faithful earnestness with which a holy Christian Church pleads on behalf of her poor departing children that God would vouchsafe to them the last great privilege and distinction possible on a death-bed, viz., the opportunity of untroubled preparation for facing this mighty trial. Sudden death, as a mere variety in the modes of dying, where death in some shape is inevitable, proposes a question of choice which, equally in the Roman and the Christian sense, will be variously answered, according to each man's variety of temperament. Meantime, one aspect of sudden death there is, one modification, upon which no doubt can arise, that of all martyrdoms it is the most agitating; viz., where it surprises a man under circumstances which offer (or which seem to offer) some hurrying, flying, inappreciably minute chance of evading it. Sudden as the danger which it affronts must be any effort by which such an evasion can be accomplished. Even *that*, even the sickening necessity for hurrying in extremity where all hurry seems destined to be vain, even that anguish is liable to a hideous exasperation in one particular case; viz., where the appeal is made not exclusively to the instinct of self-preservation, but to the conscience, on behalf of some other life besides your own, accidentally thrown upon *your* protection. To fail, to collapse in a service merely your own, might seem comparatively venial; though in fact, it is far from venial. But to fail in a case where

Providence has suddenly thrown into your hands the final interests of another, a fellow-creature shuddering between the gates of life and death,— this, to a man of apprehensive conscience, would mingle the misery of an atrocious criminality with the misery of a bloody calamity. You are called upon, by the case supposed, possibly to die; but to die at the very moment when, by any even partial failure or effeminate collapse of your energies, you will be self-denounced as a murderer. You had but the twinkling of an eye for your effort, and that effort might have been unavailing; but to have risen to the level of such an effort would have rescued you, though not from dying, yet from dying as a traitor to your final and farewell duty.

The situation here contemplated exposes a dreadful ulcer, lurking far down in the depths of human nature. It is not that men generally are summoned to face such awful trials. But potentially, and in shadowy outline, such a trial is moving subterraneously in perhaps all men's natures. Upon the secret mirror of our dreams such a trial is darkly projected, perhaps, to every one of us. That dream, so familiar to childhood, of meeting a lion, and, through languishing prostration in hope and the energies of hope, that constant sequel of lying down before the lion publishes the secret frailty of human nature — reveals its deep-seated falsehood to itself — records its abysmal treachery. Perhaps not one of us escapes that dream; perhaps, as by some sorrowful doom of man, that dream repeats for every one of us, through every generation, the original temptation in Eden. Every one of us, in this dream, has a bait offered to the infirm places of his own individual will; once again a snare is presented for tempting him into captivity to a luxury of ruin; once again, as in aboriginal Paradise, the man falls by his own choice; again, by infinite iteration, the ancient earth groans to Heaven, through her secret caves, over the weakness of her child. "Nature, from her seat, sighing through all her works," again "gives signs of woe that all is lost;" and again the counter-sigh is repeated to the sorrowing heavens for the endless rebellion against God. It is not without probability that in the world of dreams every one of us ratifies for himself the original transgression. In dreams, perhaps under some secret conflict of the midnight sleeper, lighted up to the consciousness at the time, but darkened to the memory as soon as all is finished, each several child of our mysterious race completes for himself the treason of the aboriginal fall.

The incident, so memorable in itself by its features of horror, and so scenical by its grouping for the eye, which furnished the text for this reverie upon SUDDEN DEATH occurred to myself in the dead of night, as a solitary spectator, when seated on the box of the Manchester and Glasgow mail, in the second or third summer after Waterloo. I find it necessary to relate the circumstances, because they are such as could not have occurred unless under a singular combination of accidents. In those days, the oblique and lateral communications with many rural post-offices were so arranged, either through necessity or through defect of system, as to make it requisite for the main northwestern mail (i. e., the *down* mail), on reaching Manchester, to halt for a number of hours; how many, I do not remember, — six or seven, I think; but the result was, that, in the ordinary course, the mail recommenced its journey northwards about

midnight. Wearied with the long detention at a
gloomy hotel, I walked out about eleven o'clock at
night for the sake of fresh air, meaning to fall in with
the mail and resume my seat at the post-office. The
night, however, being yet dark, as the moon had
scarcely risen, and the streets being at that hour empty
so as to offer no opportunities for asking the road,
I lost my way; and did not reach the post-office until
it was considerably past midnight; but, to my great
relief (as it was important for me to be in Westmoreland by the morning), I saw in the huge saucer eyes
of the mail, blazing through the gloom, an evidence
that my chance was not yet lost. Past the time it
was, but, by some rare accident, the mail was not
even yet ready to start. I ascended to my seat on
the box, where my cloak was still lying as it had
lain at the Bridgewater Arms. I had left it there in
imitation of a nautical discoverer, who leaves a bit
of bunting on the shore of his discovery, by way of
warning off the ground the whole human race and
notifying to the Christian and the heathen worlds,
with his best compliments, that he has hoisted
his pocket-handkerchief once and forever upon that
virgin soil; thenceforward claiming the *jus dominii*[1]
to the top of the atmosphere above it, and also the
right of driving shafts to the centre of the earth below
it; so that all people found after this warning, either
aloft in upper chambers of the atmosphere, or grop-
ing in subterraneous shafts, or squatting audaciously
on the surface of the soil, will be treated as tres-
passers, — kicked, that is to say, or decapitated, as
circumstances may suggest, by their very faithful servant, the owner of the said pocket-handkerchief. In the present case, it is probable that my

cloak might not have been respected, and the *jus gentium* [2] might have been cruelly violated in my person — for, in the dark, people commit deeds of darkness, gas being a great ally of morality — but it so happened that on this night there was no other outside passenger; and thus the crime, which else was but too probable, missed fire for want of a criminal.

Having mounted the box, I took a small quantity of laudanum, having already travelled two hundred and fifty miles, — viz., from a point seventy miles beyond London. In the taking of laudanum there was nothing extraordinary. But by accident it drew upon me the special attention of my assessor on the box, the coachman. And in *that* also there was nothing extraordinary. But by accident, and with great delight, it drew my own attention to the fact that this coachman was a monster in point of bulk, and that he had but one eye. In fact, he had been foretold by Virgil as

"Monstrum, horrendum, informe, ingens, cui lumen ademptum." [3]

He answered to the conditions in every one of the items: — 1, a monster he was; 2, dreadful; 3, shapeless; 4, huge; 5, who had lost an eye. But why should *that* delight me? Had he been one of the Calendars [4] in the *Arabian Nights*, and had paid down his eye as the price of his criminal curiosity, what right had *I* to exult in his misfortune? I did *not* exult; I delighted in no man's punishment, though it were even merited. But these personal distinctions (Nos. 1, 2, 3, 4, 5) identified in an instant an old friend of mine whom I had known in the south for some years as the most masterly of mail-coachmen. He was the man in all Europe that could (if *any* could) have driven

six-in-hand full gallop over *Al Sirat* [5] — that dreadful
bridge of Mahomet, with no side battlements, and of
extra room not enough for a razor's edge — leading
right across the bottomless gulf.   Under this eminent
man, whom in Greek I cognominated Cyclops
Diphrélates (Cyclops the Charioteer), I, and others
known to me, studied the diphrelatic art.   Excuse,
reader, a word too elegant to be pedantic.   As a
pupil, though I paid extra fees, it is to be lamented
that I did not stand high in his esteem.   It showed
his dogged honesty (though, observe, not his dis-
cernment) that he could not see my merits.   Let
us excuse his absurdity in this particular by remember-
ing his want of an eye.   Doubtless *that* made him
blind to my merits.   In the art of conversation,
however, he admitted that I had the whip-hand of
him.   On the present occasion great joy was at
our meeting.   But what was Cyclops doing here?
Had the medical men recommended northern air,
or how?   I collected, from such explanations as he
volunteered, that he had an interest at stake in some
suit-at-law now pending at Lancaster; so that probably he had got himself transferred to this station
for the purpose of connecting with his professional
pursuits an instant readiness for the calls of his
lawsuit.

Meantime, what are we stopping for?   Surely we
have now waited long enough.   Oh, this proscratinat-
ing mail, and this procrastinating post-office!   Can't
they take a lesson upon that subject from *me?*
Some people have called *me* procrastinating.   Yet
you are witness, reader, that I was kept here waiting
for the post-office.   Will the post-office lay its hand
on its heart, in its moments of sobriety, and assert

that ever it waited for me? What are they about? The guard tells me that there is a large extra accumulation of foreign mails this night, owing to irregularities caused by war, by wind, by weather, in the packet service, which as yet does not benefit at all by steam. For an *extra* hour, it seems, the post-office has been engaged in threshing out the pure wheaten correspondence of Glasgow, and winnowing it from the chaff of all baser intermediate towns. But at last all is finished. Sound your horn, guard. Manchester, good-bye; we've lost an hour by your criminal conduct at the post-office; which, however, though I do not mean to part with a serviceable ground of complaint, and one which really *is* such for the horses, to me secretly is an advantage, since it compels us to look sharply for this lost hour amongst the next eight or nine, and to recover it (if we can) at the rate of one mile extra per hour. Off we are at last, and at eleven miles per hour; and for the moment I detect no changes in the energy or in the skill of Cyclops.

From Manchester to Kendal, which virtually (though not in law) is the capital of Westmoreland there were at this time seven stages of eleven miles each. The first five of these, counting from Manchester, terminate in Lancaster, which is therefore fifty-five miles north of Manchester, and the same distance exactly from Liverpool. The first three stages terminate in Preston (called, by way of distinction from other towns of that name, *proud* Preston), at which place it is that the separate roads from Liverpool and from Manchester to the north become confluent. Within these first three stages lay the foundation, the progress, and termination of

our night's adventure. During the first stage, I
found out that Cyclops was mortal: he was liable to
the shocking affection of sleep — a thing which pre-
viously I had never suspected. If a man indulges
in the vicious habit of sleeping, all the skill in aurigation[6] of Apollo himself, with the horses of Aurora
to execute his notions, avails him nothing. "Oh,
Cyclops!" I exclaimed, "thou art mortal. My
friend, thou snorest." Through the first eleven
miles, however, this infirmity — which I grieve to
say that he shared with the whole Pagan Pantheon[7]
— betrayed itself only by brief snatches. On waking
up, he made an apology for himself which, instead
of mending matters, laid open a gloomy vista of
coming disasters. The summer assizes, he reminded
me, were now going on at Lancaster: in consequence
of which for three nights and three days he had not
lain down on a bed. During the day he was waiting
for his own summons as a witness on the trial in which
he was interested, or else, lest he should be missing
at the critical moment, was drinking with the other
witnesses under the pastoral surveillance of the at-
torneys. During the night, or that part of it which
at sea would form the middle watch, he was driving.
This explanation certainly accounted for his drowsi-
ness, but in a way which made it much more alarming; since now, after several days' resistance to this
infirmity, at length he was steadily giving way.
Throughout the second stage he grew more and more
drowsy. In the second mile of the third stage he sur-
rendered himself finally and without a struggle to
his perilous temptation. All his past resistance had
but deepened the weight of this final oppression.
Seven atmospheres of sleep rested upon him; and, to

consummate the case, our worthy guard, after singing "Love amongst the Roses" for perhaps thirty
times, without invitation and without applause,
had in revenge moodily resigned himself to slumber
— not so deep, doubtless, as the coachman's, but
deep enough for mischief. And thus at last, about
ten miles from Preston, it came about that I found
myself left in charge of His Majesty's London and
Glasgow mail, then running at the least twelve
miles an hour.

What made this negligence less criminal than else
it must have been thought was the condition of the
roads at night during the assizes. At that time, all
the law business of populous Liverpool, and also of
populous Manchester, with its vast cincture of populous rural districts, was called up by ancient usage
to the tribunal of Lilliputian Lancaster. To break
up this old traditional usage required, 1, a conflict
with powerful established interests, 2, a large system
of new arrangements, and 3, a new parliamentary
statute. But as yet this change was merely in contemplation. As things were at present, twice in the year
so vast a body of business rolled northwards from the
southern quarter of the country that for a fortnight
at least it occupied the severe exertions of two judges
in its despatch. The consequence of this was that
every horse available for such a service, along the
whole line of road, was exhausted in carrying down the
multitudes of people who were parties to the different
suits. By sunset, therefore, it usually happened that,
through utter exhaustion amongst men and horses,
the road sank into profound silence. Except the
exhaustion in the vast adjacent county of York
from a contested election, no such silence succeed-

ing to no such fiery uproar was ever witnessed in England.

On this occasion the usual silence and solitude prevailed along the road. Not a hoof nor a wheel was to be heard. And to strengthen this false luxurious confidence in the noiseless roads, it happened also that the night was one of peculiar solemnity and peace. For my own part, though slightly alive to the possibilities of peril, I had so far yielded to the influence of the mighty calm as to sink into a profound reverie. The month was August, in the middle of which lay my own birthday — a festival to every thoughtful man suggesting solemn and often sigh-born thoughts. The county was my own native county — upon which, in its southern section, more than upon any equal area known to man past or present, had descended the original curse of labor in its heaviest form, not mastering the bodies only of men as of slaves, or criminals in mines, but working through the fiery will. Upon no equal space of earth was, or ever had been, the same energy of human power put forth daily. At this particular season also of the assizes, that dreadful hurricane of flight and pursuit, as it might have seemed to a stranger, which swept to and from Lancaster all day long, hunting the county up and down, and regularly subsiding back into silence about sunset, could not fail (when·united with this permanent distinction of Lancashire as the very metropolis and citadel of labour) to point the thoughts pathetically upon that counter vision of rest, of saintly repose from strife and sorrow, towards which, as to their secret haven, the profounder aspirations of man's heart are in solitude continually travelling. Obliquely upon our

left we were nearing the sea, which also must, under
the present circumstances, be repeating the general
state of halcyon repose. The sea, the atmosphere, the
light, bore each an orchestral part in this universal lull. Moonlight and the first timid tremblings
of the dawn were by this time blending; and the
blendings were brought into a still more exquisite
state of unity by a slight silvery mist, motionless
and dreamy, that covered the woods and fields, but
with a veil of equable transparency. Except the
feet of our own horses, which, running on a sandy
margin of the road, made but little disturbance, there
was no sound abroad. In the clouds and on the
earth prevailed the same majestic peace; and, in
spite of all that the villain of a schoolmaster has done
for the ruin of our sublimer thoughts, which are the
thoughts of our infancy, we still believe in no such
nonsense as a limited atmosphere. Whatever we·
may swear with our false feigning lips, in our faithful hearts we still believe, and must for ever believe,
in fields of air traversing the total gulf between earth
and the central heavens. Still, in the confidence of
children that tread without fear *every* chamber in their
father's house, and to whom no door is closed, we,
in that Sabbatic vision which sometimes is revealed
for an hour upon nights like this, ascend with easy
steps from the sorrow-stricken fields of earth upwards
to the sandals of God.

Suddenly, from thoughts like these I was awakened
to a sullen sound, as of some motion on the distant
road. It stole upon the air for a moment; I listened
in awe; but then it died away. Once roused, however,
I could not but observe with alarm the quickened
motion of our horses. Ten years' experience had made

my eye learned in the valuing of motion; and I saw
that we were now running thirteen miles an hour.
I pretend to no presence or mind. On the contrary,
my fear is that I am miserably and shamefully
deficient in that quality as regards action. The palsy
of doubt and distraction hangs like some guilty weight
of dark unfathomed remembrances upon my energies
when the signal is flying for *action*. But, on the other
hand, this accursed gift I have, as regards *thought*,
that in the first step towards the possibility of a
misfortune I see its total evolution; in the radix of
the series I see too certainly and too instantly its
entire expansion; in the first syllable of the dreadful
sentence, I read already the last. It was not that
I feared for ourselves. *Us*, our bulk and impetus
charmed against peril in any collision. And I had
ridden through too many hundreds of perils that
were frightful to approach, that were matter of laughter to look back upon,— the first face of which was
horror, the parting face a jest,— for any anxiety to
rest upon *our* interests. The mail was not built,
I felt assured, nor bespoke, that could betray *me*
who trusted to its protection. But any carriage that
we could meet would be frail and light in comparison
of ourselves. And I remark this ominous accident of
our situation. We were on the wrong side of the
road.[8] But then, it may be said, the other party,
if other there was, might also be on the wrong side;
and two wrongs might make a right. *That* was
not likely. The same motive which had drawn *us*
to the right-hand side of the road — viz., the luxury
of the soft beaten sand, as contrasted with the
paved center — would prove attractive to others.
The two adverse carriages would therefore, to a cer-

tainty, be travelling on the same side; and from this side, as not being ours in law, the crossing over to the other would, of course, be looked for from *us*. Our lamps, still lighted, would give the impression of vigilance on our part. And every creature that met us, would rely upon *us* for quartering.[9] All this, and if the separate links of the anticipation had been a thousand times more, I saw, not discursively, or by effort, or by succession, but by one flash of horrid simultaneous intuition.

Under this steady though rapid anticipation of the evil which *might* be gathering ahead, ah! what a sullen mystery of fear, what a sigh of woe, was that which stole upon the air, as again the far-off sound of a wheel was heard? A whisper it was — a whisper from, perhaps, four miles off — secretly announcing ruin that, being foreseen, was not the less inevitable; that, being known, was not, therefore, healed. What could be done — who was it that could do it — to check the storm-flight of these maniacal horses? Could I not seize the reins from the grasp of the slumbering coachman? You, reader, think that it would have been in *your* power to do so. And I quarrel not with your estimate of yourself. But, from the way in which the coachman's hand was viced between his upper and lower thigh, this was impossible. Easy, was it? See, then, that bronze equestrian statue. The cruel rider has kept the bit in his horse's mouth for two centuries. Unbridle him for a minute, if you please, and wash his mouth with water. Easy was it? Unhorse me, then, that imperial rider; knock me those marble feet from those marble stirrups of Charlemagne.

The sounds ahead strengthened, and were now too

clearly the sounds of wheels. Who and what could it be? Was it industry in a taxed cart? Was it youthful gaiety in a gig? Was it sorrow that loitered, or joy that raced? For as yet the snatches of sound were too intermitting, from distance, to decipher the character of the motion. Whoever were the travellers, something must be done to warn them. Upon the other party rests the active responsibility, but upon *us* — and woe is me! that *us* was reduced to my frail opium-shattered self — rests the responsibility of warning. Yet, how should this be accomplished? Might I not sound the guard's horn? Already, on the first thought, I was making my way over the roof of the guard's seat. But this, from the accident which I have mentioned, of the foreign mails being piled upon the roof, was a difficult and even dangerous attempt to one cramped by nearly three hundred miles of outside travelling. And, fortunately, before I had lost much time in the attempt, our frantic horses swept round an angle of the road which opened upon us that final stage where the collision must be accomplished and the catastrophe sealed. All was apparently finished. The court was sitting; the case was heard; the judge had finished; and only the verdict was yet in arrear.

Before us lay an avenue straight as an arrow, six hundred yards, perhaps, in length; and the umbrageous trees, which rose in a regular line from either side, meeting high overhead, gave to it the character of a cathedral aisle. These trees lent a deeper solemnity to the early light; but there was still light enough to perceive, at the further end of this Gothic aisle, a frail reedy gig, in which were seated a young man, and by his side a young lady. Ah,

young sir! what are you about? If it is requisite that
you should whisper your communication to this young
lady — though really I see nobody, at an hour and
on a road so solitary, likely to overhear you — is it
therefore requisite that you should carry your lips
forward to hers? The little carriage is creeping on at
one mile an hour; and the parties within it, being thus
tenderly engaged, are naturally bending down their
heads. Between them and eternity, to all human
calculation, there is but a minute and a half. Oh
heavens! what is it that I shall do? Speaking or
acting, what help can I offer? Strange it is, and
to a mere auditor of the tale might seem laughable,
that I should need a suggestion from the *Iliad* to
prompt the sole resource that remained. Yet so it was.
Suddenly I remember the shout of Achilles, and its
effect. But could I pretend to shout like the son of
Peleus, aided by Pallas? No: but then I needed not
the shout that should alarm all Asia militant; such
a shout would suffice as might carry terror into the
hearts of two thoughtless young people and one
gig-horse. I shouted — and the young man heard
me not. A second time I shouted — and now he
heard me, for now he raised his head.

Here, then, all had been done that, by me, *could*
be done; more on *my* part was not possible. Mine
had been the first step; the second was for the young
man; the third was for God. If, said I, this stranger
is a brave man, and if indeed he loves the young girl
at his side — or, loving her not, if he feels the obligation, pressing upon every man worthy to be called
a man, of doing his utmost for a woman confided to
his protection — he will at least make some effort
to save her. If *that* fails, he will not perish the more,

or by a death more cruel, for having made it; and he
will die as brave man should, with his face to the
danger, and with his arm about the woman that he
sought in vain to save. But, if he makes no effort,
— shrinking without a struggle from his duty, — he
himself will not the less certainly perish for this
baseness of poltroonery. He will die no less: and why
not? Wherefore should we grieve that there is one
craven less in the world? No; *let* him perish, without a
pity thought of ours wasted upon him; and, in that
case, all our grief will be reserved for the fate of the
helpless girl who now, upon the least shadow of failure
in him, must, by the fiercest of translations — must,
without time for a prayer — must, within seventy
seconds, stand before the judgment-seat of God.

But craven he was not: sudden had been the call
upon him, and sudden was his answer to the call.
He saw, he heard, he comprehended the ruin that
was coming down: already its gloomy shadow darkened above him; and already he was measuring his
strength to deal with it. Ah! what a vulgar thing
does courage seem, when we see nations buying it
and selling it for a shilling a day;[10] ah! what a sublime thing does courage seem, when some fearful
summons on the great deeps of life carries a man, as
if running before a hurricane, up to the giddy crest
of some tumultuous crisis from which lie two courses,
and a voice says to him audibly, "One way lies hope;
take the other, and mourn forever!" How grand
a triumph, if, even then, amidst the raving of all
around him, and the frenzy of the danger, the man
is able to confront his situation,— is able to retire for
a moment into solitude with God, and to seek his
counsel for *Him!*

For seven seconds, it might be, of his seventy the stranger settled his countenance steadfastly upon us, as if to search and value every element in the conflict before him. For five seconds more of his seventy he sat immovably, like one that mused on some great purpose. For five more, perhaps, he sat with eyes upraised, like one that prayed in sorrow, under some extremity of doubt, for light that should guide him to the better choice. Then suddenly he rose; stood upright; and by a powerful strain upon the reins, raising his horse's fore-feet from the ground, he slewed him round on the pivot of his hind-legs, so as to plant the little equipage in a position nearly at right angles to ours. Thus far his condition was not improved, except as a first step had been taken towards the possibility of a second. If no more were done, nothing was done; for the little carriage still occupied the very centre of our path, though in an altered direction. Yet even now·it may not be too late; fifteen of the seventy seconds may still be unexhausted; and one almighty bound may avail to clear the ground. Hurry then, hurry! for the flying moments — *they* hurry. Oh, hurry, hurry, my brave young man! for the cruel hoofs of our horses — *they* also hurry! Fast are the flying moments, faster are the hoofs of our horses. But fear not for *him*, if human energy can suffice; faithful was he that drove to his terrific duty; faithful was the horse to *his* command. One blow, one impulse given with voice and hand, by the stranger, one rush from the horse, one bound as if in the act of rising to a fence, landed the docile creature's fore-feet upon the crown or arching centre of the road. The larger half of the little equipage had then cleared our overtowering shadow: *that* was evident even to my own agitated sight. But it mattered little that one wreck should float off in safety if upon the wreck that perished were embarked the human freightage. The rear part of the carriage — was *that* certainly beyond the line of absolute ruin? What power could answer the question? Glance of eye, thought of man, wing of angel, which of these had speed enough to sweep between the question and the answer, and divide the one from the other? Light does not tread upon the steps of light more indivisibly than did our all-conquering arrival upon the escaping efforts of the gig. *That* must the young man have felt too plainly. His back was now turned to us; not by sight could he any longer communicate with the peril; but, by the dreadful rattle of our harness, too truly had his ear been instructed that all was finished as regarded any effort of *his*. Already in resignation he had rested from his struggle; and perhaps in his heart he was whispering, "Father, which art in heaven, do Thou finish above what I on earth have attempted." Faster than ever millrace we ran past them in our inexorable flight. Oh, raving of hurricanes that must have sounded in their young ears at the moment of our transit! Even in that moment the thunder of collision spoke aloud. Either with the swingle-bar or with the haunch of our near leader, we had struck off the wheel of the little gig, which stood rather obliquely and not quite so far advanced as to be accurately parallel with the near wheel. The blow, from the fury of our passage, resounded terrifically. I rose in horror to gaze upon the ruins we might have caused. From my elevated station I looked down, and looked back upon the scene, which in a moment told its own tale, and wrote all its records on my heart forever.

Here was the map of the passion that now had finished. The horse was planted immovably, with his fore-feet upon the paved crest of the central road. He of the whole party might be supposed untouched by the passion of death. The little cany carriage — partly, perhaps, from the violent torsion of the wheels in its recent movement, partly from the thundering blow we had given to it — as if it sympathized with human horror, was all alive with tremblings and shiverings. The young man trembled not, nor shivered. He sat like a rock. But *his* was the steadiness of agitation frozen into rest by horror. As yet he dared not to look around; for he knew that, if anything remained to do, by him it could no longer be done. And as yet he knew not for certain if their safety were accomplished. But the lady ——

But the lady ——! Oh, Heavens! will that spectacle ever depart from my dreams, as she rose and sank upon her seat, sank and rose, threw up her arms wildly to heaven, clutched at some visionary object in the air, fainting, praying, raving, despairing? Figure to yourself, reader, the elements of the case; suffer me to recall before your mind the circumstances of that unparalleled situation. From the silence and deep peace of this saintly summer night — from the pathetic blending of this sweet moonlight, dawnlight, dreamlight — from the manly tenderness of this flattering, whispering, murmuring love — suddenly as from the woods and fields — suddenly as from the chambers of the air opening in revelation — suddenly as from the ground yawning at her feet, leaped upon her, with the flashing of cataracts, Death the crowned phantom, with all the equipage of his terrors, and the tiger roar of his voice.

The moments were numbered; the strife was finished; the vision was closed. In the twinkling of an eye, our flying horses had carried us to the termination of the umbrageous aisle; at the right angles we wheeled into our former direction; the turn of the road carried the scene out of my eyes in an instant, and swept it into my dreams forever.

COMPENSATION

THE wings of Time are black and white,
Pied with morning and with night.
Mountain tall and ocean deep
Trembling balance duly keep.
In changing moon, in tidal wave,
Glows the feud of Want and Have.
Gauge of more and less through space
Electric star and pencil plays.
The lonely Earth amid the balls.
That hurry through the eternal halls,
A makeweight flying to the void,
Supplemental asteroid,
Or compensatory spark,
Shoots across the neutral Dark.[1]

MAN's the elm, and Wealth the vine,
Stanch and strong the tendrils twine:
Though the frail ringlets thee deceive,
None from its stock that vine can reave.
Fear not, then, thou child infirm,
There's no god dare wrong a worm.
Laurel crowns cleave to deserts
And power to him who power exerts;
Hast not thy share? On wingèd feet,
Lo! it rushes thee to meet;
And all that Nature made thy own,
Floating in air or pent in stone,
Will rive the hills and swim the sea
And, like thy shadow, follow thee.

RALPH WALDO EMERSON

COMPENSATION

Ever since I was a boy I have wished to write a discourse on Compensation; for it seemed to me when very young that on this subject life was ahead of theology and the people knew more than the preachers taught. The documents too from which the doctrine is to be drawn, charmed my fancy by their endless variety, and lay always before me, even in sleep; for they are the tools in our hands, the bread in our basket, the transactions of the street, the farm and the dwelling-house; greetings, relations, debts and credits, the influence of character, the nature and endowment of all men. It seemed to me also that in it might be shown men a ray of divinity, the present action of the soul of this world, clean from all vestige of tradition; and so the heart of man might be bathed by an inundation of eternal love, conversing with that which he knows was always and always must be, because it really is now. It appeared moreover that if this doctrine could be stated in terms with any resemblance to those bright intuitions in which this truth is sometimes revealed to us, it would be a star in many dark hours and crooked passages in our journey, that would not suffer us to lose our way.

I was lately confirmed in these desires by hearing a sermon at church. The preacher, a man esteemed for his orthodoxy, unfolded in the ordinary manner the doctrine of the Last Judgment. He assumed that judgment is not executed in this world; that the wicked are successful; that the good are miserable; and then urged from reason and from Scripture a compensation to be made to both parties in the next life. No offence appeared to be taken by the congregation at this doctrine. As far as I could observe when the meeting broke up they separated without remark on the sermon.

Yet what was the import of this teaching? What did the preacher mean by saying that the good are miserable in the present life? Was it that houses and lands, offices, wine, horses, dress, luxury, are had by unprincipled men, whilst the saints are poor and despised; and that a compensation is to be made to these last hereafter, by giving them the like gratifications another day, — bank-stock and doubloons, venison and champagne? This must be the compensation intended; for what else? Is it that they are to have leave to pray and praise? to love and serve men? Why, that they can do now. The legitimate inference the disciple would draw was,— "We are to have *such* a good time as the sinners have now;"— or, to push it to its extreme import, — "You sin now, we shall sin by and by; we would sin now, if we could; not being successful we expect our revenge to-morrow."

The fallacy lay in the immense concession that the bad are successful; that justice is not done now. The blindness of the preacher consisted in deferring to the base estimate of the market of what constitutes a manly success, instead of confronting and convicting the world from the truth; announcing the presence of the soul; the omnipotence of the will; and so establishing the standard of good and ill, of success and falsehood.

I find a similar base tone in the popular religious works of the day and the same doctrines assumed by the literary men when occasionally they treat the related topics. I think that our popular theology has gained in decorum, and not in principle, over the susperstitions it has displaced. But men are better than their theology. Their daily life gives it the lie. Every ingenuous and aspiring soul leaves the doctrine behind him in his own experience, and all men feel sometimes the falsehood which they cannot demonstrate. For men are wiser than they know. That which they hear in schools and pulpits without afterthought, if said in conversation would probably be questioned in silence. If a man dogmatize in a mixed company on Providence and the divine laws, is he answered by a silence which conveys well enough to an observer the dissatisfaction of the hearer, but his incapacity to make his own statement.

I shall attempt in this and the following chapter [2] to record some facts that indicate the path of the law of Compensation; happy beyond my expectation if I shall truly draw the smallest arc of this circle.

Polarity, or action and reaction, we meet in every part of nature; in darkness and light; in heat and cold; in the ebb and flow of waters; in male and female; in the inspiration and expiration of plants and animals; in the equation of quantity and quality in the fluids of the animal body; in the systole and diastole of the heart; in the undulations of fluids and of sound; in the centrifugal and centripetal gravity; in electricity,

galvanism, and chemical affinity. Superinduce magnetism at one end of a needle, the opposite magnetism takes place at the other end. If the south
attracts, the north repels. To empty here, you must
condense there. An inevitable dualism bisects nature,
so that each thing is a half, and suggests another
thing to make it whole; as, spirit, matter; man,
woman; odd, even; subjective, objective; in, out;
upper, under; motion, rest; yea, nay.

Whilst the world is thus dual, so is every one of
its parts. The entire system of things gets represented
in every particle. There is somewhat that resembles
the ebb and flow of the sea, day and night, man and
woman, in a single needle of the pine, in a kernel of
corn, in each individual of every animal tribe. The
reaction, so grand in the elements, is repeated within
these small boundaries. For example, in the animal
kingdom the physiologist has observed that no creatures are favourites, but a certain compensation
balances every gift and every defect. A surplusage
given to one part is paid out of a reduction from
another part of the same creature. If the head and
neck are enlarged, the trunk and extremities are cut
short.

The theory of the mechanic forces is another example. What we gain in power is lost in time, and the
converse. The periodic or compensating errors of the
planets is another instance. The influences of climate and soil in political history is another. The
cold climate invigorates. The barren soil does not
breed fevers, crocodiles, tigers or scorpions.

The same dualism underlies the nature and condition of man. Every excess causes a defect; every defect an excess. Every sweet hath its sour; every evil

its good. Every faculty which is a receiver of pleasure has an equal penalty put on its abuse. It is to answer for its moderation with its life. For every grain of wit there is a grain of folly. For every thing you have missed, you have gained something else; and for every thing you gain, you lose something. If riches increase, they are increased that use them. If the gatherer gathers too much, Nature takes out of the man what she puts into his chest; swells the estate, but kills the owner. Nature hates monopolies and exceptions. The waves of the sea do not more speedily seek a level from their loftiest tossing than the varieties of condition tend to equalize themselves. There is always some levelling circumstance that puts down the overbearing, the strong, the rich, the fortunate, substantially on the same ground with all others. Is a man too strong and fierce for society and by temper and position a bad citizen, — a morose ruffian, with a dash of the pirate in him? — Nature sends him a troop of pretty sons and daughters who are getting along in the dame's classes at the village school, and love and fear for them smooths his grim scowl to courtesy. Thus she contrives to intenerate the granite and felspar, takes the boar out and puts the lamb in and keeps her balance true.

The farmer imagines power and place are fine things. But the President has paid dear for his White House. It has commonly cost him all his peace, and the best of his manly attributes. To preserve for a short time so conspicuous an appearance before the world, he is content to eat dust before the real masters who stand erect behind the throne. Or do men desire the more substantial and permanent grandeur of genius? Neither has this an immunity. He who by force of will or of thought is great and overlooks thousands, has the charges of that eminence. With every influx of light comes new danger. Has he light? he must bear witness to the light and always outrun that sympathy which gives him such keen satisfaction, by his fidelity to new revelations of the incessant soul. He must hate father and mother, wife and child. Has he all that the world loves and admires and covets?— he must cast behind him their admiration and afflict them by faithfulness to his truth and become a byword and a hissing.

This law writes the laws of cities and nations. It is in vain to build or plot or combine against it. Things refuse to be mismanaged long. *Res nolunt diu male administrari.*[3] Though no checks to a new evil appear, the checks exist, and will appear. If the government is cruel, the governor's life is not safe. If you tax too high, the revenue will yield nothing. If you make the criminal code sanguinary, juries will not convict. If the law is too mild, private vengeance comes in. If the government is a terrific democracy, the pressure is resisted by an over-charge of energy in the citizen, and life glows with a fiercer flame. The true life and satisfactions of man seem to elude the utmost rigors or felicities of condition and to establish themselves with great indifferency under all varieties of circumstances. Under all governments the influence of character remains the same,— in Turkey and in New England about alike. Under the primeval despots of Egypt, history honestly confesses that man must have been as free as culture could make him.

These appearances indicate the fact that the universe is represented in every one of its particles.

Every thing in nature contains all the powers of nature. Every thing is made of one hidden stuff; as the naturalist sees one type under every metamorphosis, and regards a horse as a running man, a fish as a swimming man, a bird as a flying man, a tree as a rooted man. Each new form repeats not only the main character of the type, but part for part all the details, all the aims, furtherances, hindrances, energies, and whole system of every other. Every occupation, trade, art, transaction, is a compend of the world and a correlative of every other. Each one is an entire emblem of human life; of its good and ill, its trials, its enemies, its course and its end. And each one must somehow accommodate the whole man and recite all his destiny.

The world globes itself in a drop of dew. The microscope cannot find the animalcule which is less perfect for being little. Eyes, ears, taste, smell, motion, resistance, appetite, and organs of reproduction that take hold on eternity, — all find room to consist in the small creature. So do we put our life into every act. The true doctrine of omnipresence is that God reappears with all his parts in every moss and cobweb. The value of the universe contrives to throw itself into every point. If the good is there, so is the evil; if the affinity, so the repulsion; if the force, so the limitation.

Thus is the universe alive. All things are moral. That soul which within us is a sentiment, outside of us is a law. We feel its inspiration; but there in history we can see its fatal strength. "It is in the world, and the world was made by it." Justice is not postponed. A perfect equity adjusts its balance in all parts of life. 'Αεί γὰρ εὖ πίπτουσιν οἱ Διὸς κύβοι,[4]

— The dice of God are always loaded. The world looks like a multiplication-table, or a mathematical equation, which, turn it how you will, balances itself. Take what figure you will, its exact value, nor more nor less, still returns to you. Every secret is told, every crime is punished, every virtue rewarded, every wrong redressed, in silence and certainty. What we call retribution is the universal necessity by which the whole appears wherever a part appears. If you see smoke, there must be fire. If you see a hand or a limb, you know that the trunk to which it belongs is there behind.

Every act rewards itself, or in other words integrates itself, in a twofold manner; first in the thing, or in real nature; and secondly in the circumstance, or in apparent nature. Men call the circumstance the retribution. The causal retribution is in the thing and is seen by the soul. The retribution in the circumstance is seen by the understanding; it is inseparable from the thing, but is often spread over a long time and so does not become distinct until after many years. The specific stripes may follow late after the offence, but they follow because they accompany it. Crime and punishment grow out of one stem. Punishment is a fruit that unsuspected ripens within the flower of the pleasure which concealed it. Cause and effect, means and ends, seed and fruit, cannot be severed; for the effect already blooms in the cause, the end preëxists in the means, the fruit in the seed.

Whilst thus the world will be whole and refuses to be disparted, we seek to act partially, to sunder, to appropriate; for example, — to gratify the senses we sever the pleasure of the senses from the needs of the character. The ingenuity of man has always been dedicated to the solution of one problem, — how to detach the sensual sweet, the sensual strong, the sensual bright, etc., from the moral sweet, the moral deep, the moral fair; that is, again, to contrive to cut clean off this upper surface so thin as to leave it bottomless; to get a *one end*, without an *other end*. The soul says, "Eat;" the body would feast. The soul says, "The man and woman shall be one flesh and one soul;" the body would join the flesh only. The soul says, "Have dominion over all things to the ends of virtue;" the body would have the power over things to its own ends.

The soul strives amain to live and work through all things. It would be the only fact. All things shall be added unto it, — power, pleasure, knowledge, beauty. The particular man aims to be somebody; to set up for himself; to truck and higgle for a private good; and, in particulars, to ride that he may ride; to dress that he may be dressed; to eat that he may eat; and to govern, that he may be seen. Men seek to be great; they would have offices, wealth, power, and fame. They think that to be great is to possess one side of nature, — the sweet, without the other side, the bitter.

This dividing and detaching is steadily counteracted. Up to this day it must be owned no projector has had the smallest success. The parted water reunites behind our hand. Pleasure is taken out of pleasant things, profit out of profitable things, power out of strong things, as soon as we seek to separate them from the whole. We can no more halve things and get the sensual good, by itself, than we can get an inside that shall have no outside, or a light without a shadow. "Drive out Nature with a fork, she comes running back."

Life invests itself with inevitable conditions, which the unwise seek to dodge, which one and another brags that he does not know, that they do not touch him; — but the brag is on his lips, the conditions are in his soul. If he escapes them in one part they attack him in another more vital part. If he has escaped them in form and in the appearance, it is because he has resisted his life and fled from himself, and the retribution is so much death. So signal is the failure of all attempts to make this separation of the good from the tax, that the experiment would not be tried,— since to try it is to be mad,— but for the circumstance that when the disease begins in the will, of rebellion and separation, the intellect is at once infected, so that the man ceases to see God whole in each object, but is able to see the sensual allurement of an object and not see the sensual hurt; he sees the mermaid's head but not the dragon's tail, and thinks he can cut off that which he would have from that which he would not have. "How secret art thou who dwellest in the highest heavens in silence, O thou only great God, sprinkling with an unwearied providence certain penal blindnesses upon such as have unbridled desires!"

The human soul is true to these facts in the painting of fable, of history, of law, of proverbs, of conversation. It finds a tongue in literature unawares. Thus the Greeks called Jupiter, Supreme Mind; but having traditionally ascribed to him many base actions, they involuntarily made amends to reason by tying up the hands of so bad a god. He is made as helpless as a king of England. Prometheus knows

one secret which Jove must bargain for; Minerva,
another. He cannot get his own thunders; Minerva
keeps the key of them: —

> "Of all the gods, I only know the keys
> That ope the solid doors within whose vaults
> His thunders sleep."

A plain confession of the in-working of the All and
of its moral aim. The Indian mythology ends in the
same ethics; and it would seem impossible for any
fable to be invented and get any currency which was
not moral. Aurora forgot to ask youth for her lover,
and though Tithonus is immortal, he is old. Achilles
is not quite invulnerable; the sacred waters did not
wash the heel by which Thetis held him. Siegfried,
in the Nibelungen, is not quite immortal, for a leaf
fell on his back whilst he was bathing in the dragon's
blood, and that spot which it covered is mortal. And
so it must be. There is a crack in every thing God
has made. It would seem there is always this vin-
dictive circumstance stealing in at unawares even into
the wild poesy in which the human fancy attempted
to make bold holiday and to shake itself free of the
old laws, — this back-stroke, this kick of the gun,
certifying that the law is fatal; that in nature nothing
can be given, all things are sold.

This is that ancient doctrine of Nemesis, who keeps
watch in the universe and lets no offence go unchas-
tised. The Furies, they said, are attendants on
justice, and if the sun in heaven should transgress
his path they would punish him. The poets related
that stone walls and iron swords and leathern thongs
had an occult sympathy with the wrongs of their own-
ers; that the belt which Ajax gave Hector dragged the

Trojan hero over the field at the wheels of the car of Achilles, and the sword which Hector gave Ajax was that on whose point Ajax fell. They recorded that when the Thasians [5] erected a statue to Theagenes, a victor in the games, one of his rivals went to it by night and endeavoured to throw it down by repeated blows, until at last he moved it from its pedestal and was crushed to death beneath its fall.

This voice of fable has in it somewhat divine. It came from thought above the will of the writer. That is the best part of each writer which has nothing private in it; that which he does not know; that which flowed out of his constitution and not from his too active invention; that which in the study of a single artist you might not easily find, but in the study of many you would abstract as the spirit of them all. Phidias it is not, but the work of man in that early Hellenic world that I would know. The name and circumstance of Phidias,[6] however convenient for history, embarrass when we come to the highest criticism. We are to see that which man was tending to do in a given period, and was hindered, or, if you will, modified in doing, by the interfering volitions of Phidias, of Dante, of Shakespeare, the organ whereby man at the moment wrought.

Still more striking is the expression of this fact in the proverbs of all nations, which are always the literature of reason, or the statements of an absolute truth without qualification. Proverbs, like the sacred books of each nation, are the sanctuary of the intuitions. That which the droning world, chained to appearances, will not allow the realist to say in his own words, it will suffer him to say in proverbs without contradiction. And his law of laws, which the

pulpit, the senate, and the college deny, is hourly
preached in all markets and workshops by flights of
proverbs, whose teaching is as true and as omni-
present as that of birds and flies.

All things are double, one against another. — Tit
for tat; an eye for an eye; a tooth for a tooth; blood
for blood; measure for measure; love for love. —
Give, and it shall be given you. — He that watereth
shall be watered himself. — What will you have?
quoth God; pay for it and take it. — Nothing venture, nothing have. — Thou shalt be paid exactly
for what thou hast done, no more, no less. — Who
doth not work shall not eat. — Harm watch, harm
catch. Curses always recoil on the head of him who
imprecates them. — If you put a chain around the
neck of a slave, the other end fastens itself around
your own. — Bad counsel confounds the adviser. —
The Devil is an ass.

It is thus written, because it is thus in life. Our
action is overmastered and characterized above our
will by the law of nature. We aim at a petty end
quite aside from the public good, but our act arranges
itself by irresistible magnetism in a line with the
poles of the world.

A man cannot speak but he judges himself. With
his will or against his will he draws his portrait to
the eye of his companions by every word. Every
opinion reacts on him who utters it. It is a thread-
ball thrown at a mark, but the other end remains in
the thrower's bag. Or rather it is a harpoon hurled
at the whale, unwinding, as it flies, a coil of cord in
the boat, and, if the harpoon is not good, or not well
thrown, it will go nigh to cut the steersman in twain
or to sink the boat.

You cannot do wrong without suffering wrong. "No man had ever a point of pride that was not injurious to him," said Burke. The exclusive in fashionable life does not see that he excludes himself from enjoyment, in the attempt to appropriate it. The exclusionist in religion does not see that he shuts the door of heaven on himself, in striving to shut out others. Treat men as pawns and ninepins and you shall suffer as well as they. If you leave out their heart, you shall lose your own. The senses would make things of all persons; of women, of children, of the poor. The vulgar proverb, "I will get it from his purse or get it from his skin," is sound philosophy.

All infractions of love and equity in our social relations are speedily punished. They are punished by fear. Whilst I stand in simple relations to my fellow man, I have no displeasure in meeting him. We meet as water meets water, or as two currents of air mix, with perfect diffusion and interpenetration of nature. But as soon as there is any departure from simplicity and attempt at halfness, or good for me that is not good for him, my neighbor feels the wrong; he shrinks from me as far as I have shrunk from him; his eyes no longer seek mine; there is war between us; there is hate in him and fear in me.

All the old abuses in society, universal and particular, all unjust accumulations of property and power, are avenged in the same manner. Fear is an instructor of great sagacity and the herald of all revolutions. One thing he teaches, that there is rottenness where he appears. He is a carrion crow, and though you see not well what he hovers for, there is death somewhere. Our property is timid, our laws are timid, our cultivated classes are timid. Fear for ages has boded and mowed and gibbered over government and property. That obscene bird is not there for nothing. He indicates great wrongs which must be revised.

Of the like nature is that expectation of change which instantly follows the suspension of our voluntary activity. The terror of cloudless noon, the emerald of Polycrates,[7] the awe of prosperity, the instinct which leads every generous soul to impose on itself tasks of a noble asceticism and vicarious virtue, are the tremblings of the balance of justice through the heart and mind of man.

Experienced men of the world know very well that it is best to pay scot and lot as they go along, and that a man often pays dear for a small frugality. The borrower runs in his own debt. Has a man gained any thing who has received a hundred favours and rendered none? Has he gained by borrowing, through indolence or cunning, his neighbour's wares, or horses, or money? There arises on the deed the instant acknowledgment of benefit on the one part and of debt on the other; that is, of superiority and inferiority. The transaction remains in the memory of himself and his neighbour; and every new transaction alters according to its nature their relation to each other. He may soon come to see that he had better have broken his own bones than to have ridden in his neighbour's coach, and that "the highest price he can pay for a thing is to ask for it."

A wise man will extend this lesson to all parts of life, and know that it is the part of prudence to face every claimant and pay every just demand on your time, your talents, or your heart. Always pay; for first or last you must pay your entire debt. Persons and events may stand for a time between you and justice, but it is only a postponement. You must pay at last your own debt. If you are wise you will dread a prosperity which only loads you with more. Benefit is the end of nature. But for every benefit which you receive, a tax is levied. He is great who confers the most benefits. He is base, — and that is the one base thing in the universe, — to receive favours and render none. In the order of nature we cannot render benefits to those from whom we receive them, or only seldom. But the benefit we receive must be rendered again, line for line, deed for deed, cent for cent, to somebody. Beware of too much good staying in your hand. It will fast corrupt and worm worms. Pay it away quickly in some sort.

Labour is watched over by the same pitiless laws. Cheapest, say the prudent, is the dearest labour. What we buy in a broom, a mat, a wagon, a knife, is some application of good sense to a common want. It is best to pay in your land a skilful gardener, or to buy good sense applied to gardening; in your sailor, good sense applied to navigation; in the house, good sense applied to cooking, sewing, serving; in your agent, good sense applied to accounts and affairs. So do you multiply your presence, or spread yourself throughout your estate. But because of the dual constitution of things, in labour as in life there can be no cheating. The thief steals from himself. The swindler swindles himself. For the real price of labour is knowledge and virtue, whereof wealth and credit are signs. These signs, like paper money, may be counterfeited or stolen, but that which they represent namely, knowledge and virtue, cannot be counterfeited or stolen. These ends of labour cannot be answered but by real exertions of the mind, and in obedience to pure motives. The cheat, the defaulter, the gambler, cannot extort the knowledge of material and moral nature which his honest care and pains yield to the operative. The law of Nature is, Do the thing, and you shall have the power; but they who do not the thing have not the power.

Human labour, through all its forms, from the sharpening of a stake to the construction of a city or an epic, is one immense illustration of the perfect compensation of the universe. The absolute balance of Give and Take, the doctrine that every thing has its price, — and if that price is not paid, not that thing but something else is obtained, and that it is impossible to get anything without its price, — is not less sublime in the columns of a leger [8] than in the budgets of states, in the laws of light and darkness, in all the action and reaction of nature. I cannot doubt that the high laws which each man sees implicated in those processes with which he is conversant, the stern ethics which sparkle on his chisel-edge, which are measured out by his plumb and foot-rule, which stand as manifest in the footing of the shop-bill as in the history of a state,— do recommend to him his trade, and though seldom named, exalt his business to his imagination.

The league between virtue and nature engages all things to assume a hostile front to vice. The beautiful laws and substances of the world persecute and whip the traitor. He finds that things are arranged for truth and benefit, but there is no den in the wide world to hide a rogue. Commit a crime, and the earth is made of glass. Commit a crime, and it seems as if a coat of snow fell on the ground, such as reveals

in the woods the track of every partridge and fox
and squirrel and mole. You cannot recall the spoken
word, you cannot wipe out the foot-track, you cannot
draw up the ladder, so as to leave no inlet or clew.
Some damning circumstance always transpires. The
laws and substances of nature — water, snow, wind,
gravitation — become penalties to the thief.

On the other hand the law holds with equal sureness
for all right action. Love, and you shall be loved.
All love is mathematically just, as much as the
two sides of an algebraic equation. The good man
has absolute good, which like fire turns every thing
to its own nature, so that you cannot do him any harm;
but as the royal armies sent against Napoleon, when
he approached cast down their colours and from enemies became friends, so disasters of all kinds, as sickness, offence, poverty, prove benefactors: —

> "Winds blow and waters roll
> Strength to the brave and power and deity,
> Yet in themselves are nothing."

The good are befriended even by weakness and
defect. As no man had ever a point of pride that was
not injurious to him, so no man had ever a defect
that was not somewhere made useful to him. The
stag in the fable admired his horns and blamed his
feet, but when the hunter came, his feet saved him,
and afterwards, caught in the thicket, his horns destroyed him. Every man in his lifetime needs to thank
his faults. As no man thoroughly understands a
truth until he has contended against it, so no man
has a thorough acquaintance with the hindrances
or talents of men until he has suffered from the
one and seen the triumph of the other over his own

want of the same. Has he a defect of temper that
unfits him to live in society? Thereby he is driven
to entertain himself alone and acquire habits of self-
help; and thus, like the wounded oyster, he mends
his shell with pearl.

Our strength grows out of our weakness. The
indignation which arms itself with secret forces does
not waken until we are pricked and stung and sorely
assailed. A great man is always willing to be little.
Whilst he sits on the cushion of advantages, he goes
to sleep. When he is pushed, tormented, defeated,
he has a chance to learn something; he has been put
on his wits, on his manhood; he has gained facts;
learns his ignorance; is cured of the insanity of conceit; has got moderation and real skill. The wise man
throws himself on the side of his assailants. It is
more his interest than it is theirs to find his weak
point. The wound cicatrizes and falls off from him
like a dead skin, and when they would triumph,
lo! he has passed on invulnerable. Blame is safer
than praise. I hate to be defended in a newspaper.
As long as all that is said is said against me, I feel a
certain assurance of success. But as soon as honeyed
words of praise are spoken for me I feel as one that
lies unprotected before his enemies. In general,
every evil to which we do not succumb is a benefac-
tor. As the Sandwich Islander believes that the
strength and valour of the enemy he kills passes into
himself, so we gain the strength of the temptation
we resist.

The same guards which protect us from disaster,
defect and enmity, defend us, if we will, from selfish-
ness and fraud. Bolts and bars are not the best of
our institutions, nor is shrewdness in trade a mark of

wisdom, Men suffer all their life long under the foolish superstition that they can be cheated. But it is
as impossible for a man to be cheated by any one
but himself, as for a thing to be and not to be at the
same time. There is a third silent party to all our
bargains. The nature and soul of things takes on
itself the guaranty of the fulfilment of every contract,
so that honest service cannot come to loss. If you
serve an ungrateful master, serve him the more.
Put God in your debt. Every stroke shall be repaid.
The longer the payment is withholden, the better
for you; for compound interest on compound interest
is the rate and usage of this exchequer.

The history of persecution is a history of endeavours
to cheat nature, to make water run up hill, to twist a
rope of sand. It makes no difference whether the
actors be many or one, a tyrant or a mob. A mob is
a society of bodies voluntarily bereaving themselves
of reason and traversing its work. The mob is man
voluntarily descending to the nature of the beast. Its
fit hour of activity is night. Its actions are insane,
like its whole constitution. It persecutes a principle;
it would whip a right; it would tar and feather justice, by inflicting fire and outrage upon the houses
and persons of those who have these. It resembles the
prank of boys, who run with fire-engines to put out the
ruddy aurora streaming to the stars. The inviolate
spirit turns their spite against the wrongdoers. The
martyr cannot be dishonoured. Every lash inflicted
is a tongue of fame; every prison a more illustrious
abode; every burned book or house enlightens
the world; every suppressed or expunged word rever-
berates through the earth from side to side. Hours
of sanity and consideration are always arriving to

communities, as to individuals, when the truth is seen and the martyrs are justified.

Thus do all things preach the indifferency of circumstances. The man is all. Every thing has two sides, a good and an evil. Every advantage has its tax. I learn to be content. But the doctrine of compensation is not the doctrine of indifferency. The thoughtless say, on hearing these representations,— What boots it to do well? there is one event to good and evil; if I gain any good I must pay for it; if I lose any good I gain some other; all actions are indifferent.

There is a deeper fact in the soul than compensation, to wit, its own nature. The soul is not a compensation, but a life. The soul *is*. Under all this running sea of circumstance, whose waters ebb and flow with perfect balance, lies the aboriginal abyss of real Being. Essence, or God, is not a relation or a part, but the whole. Being is the vast affirmative, excluding negation, self-balanced, and swallowing up all relations, parts and times within itself. Nature, truth, virtue, are the influx from thence. Vice is the absence or departure of the same. Nothing, Falsehood, may indeed stand as the great Night or shade on which as a background the living universe paints itself forth, but no fact is begotten by it; it cannot work, for it is not. It cannot work any good; it cannot work any harm. It is harm inasmuch as it is worse not to be than to be.

We feel defrauded of the retribution due to evil acts, because the criminal adheres to his vice and contumacy and does not come to a crisis or judgment anywhere in visible nature. There is no stunning confutation of his nonsense before men and angels.

Has he therefore outwitted the law? Inasmuch as he carries the malignity and the lie with him he so far deceases from nature. In some manner there will be a demonstration of the wrong to the understanding also; but should we not see it, this deadly deduction makes square the eternal account.

Neither can it be said, on the other hand, that the gain of rectitude must be bought by any loss. There is no penalty to virtue; no penalty to wisdom; they are proper additions of being. In a virtuous action I properly *am;* in a virtuous act I add to the world; I plant into deserts conquered from Chaos and Nothing and see the darkness receding on the limits of the horizon. There can be no excess to love, none to knowledge, none to beauty, when these attributes are considered in the purest sense. The soul refuses limits, and always affirms an Optimism, never a Pessimism.

His life is a progress, and not a station. His instinct is trust. Our instinct uses "more" and "less" in application to man, of the *presence of the soul,* and not of its absence; the brave man is greater than the coward; the true, the benevolent, the wise, is more a man and not less, than the fool and knave. There is no tax on the good of virtue, for that is the incoming of God himself, or absolute existence, without any comparative. Material good has its tax, and if it came without desert or sweat, has no root in me, and the next wind will blow it away. But all the good of nature is the soul's, and may be had if paid for in nature's lawful coin, that is, by labour which the heart and the head allow. I no longer wish to meet a good I do not earn, for example to find a pot of buried gold, knowing that it brings with it new

burdens. I do not wish more external goods,— neither
possessions, nor honours, nor powers, nor persons. The
gain is apparent; the tax is certain. But there is no
tax on the knowledge that the compensation exists
and that it is not desirable to dig up treasure. Herein
I rejoice with a serene eternal peace. I contract the
boundaries of possible mischief. I learn the wisdom
of St. Bernard, "Nothing can work me damage except
myself; the harm that I sustain I carry about with
me, and never am a real sufferer but by my own
fault."

In the nature of the soul is the compensation for
the inequalities of condition. The radical tragedy of
nature seems to be the distinction of More and Less.
How can Less not feel the pain; how not feel indignation or malevolence towards More? Look at those
who have less faculty, and one feels sad and knows
not well what to make of it. He almost shuns their
eye; he fears they will upbraid God. What should
they do? It seems a great injustice. But see the
facts nearly and these mountainous inequalities van-
ish. Love reduces them as the sun melts the iceberg
in the sea. The heart and soul of all men being
one, this bitterness of *His* and *Mine* ceases. His is
mine. I am my brother and my brother is me. If I
feel overshadowed and outdone by great neighbours,
I can yet love; I can still receive; and he that loveth
maketh his own the grandeur he loves. Thereby I
make the discovery that my brother is my guardian,
acting for me with the friendliest designs, and the
estate I so admired and envied is my own. It is the
nature of the soul to appropriate all things. Jesus
and Shakespeare are fragments of the soul, and by
love I conquer and incorporate them in my own con-

scious domain. His virtue,— is not that mine? His
wit, — if it cannot be made mine, it is not wit.

Such also is the natural history of calamity. The
changes which break up at short intervals the prosperity of men are advertisements of a nature whose
law is growth. Every soul is by this intrinsic necessity
quitting its whole system of things, its friends and
home and laws and faith, as the shell-fish crawls out
of its beautiful but stony case, because it no longer
admits of its growth, and slowly forms a new house.
In proportion to the vigour of the individual these
revolutions are frequent, until in some happier mind
they are incessant and all worldly relations hang very
loosely about him, becoming as it were a transparent
fluid membrane through which the living form is seen,
and not, as in most men, an indurated heterogene-
ous fabric of many dates and of no settled character
in which the man is imprisoned. Then there can be
enlargement, and the man of to-day scarcely recognizes the man of yesterday. And such should be the
outward biography of man in time, a putting off of
dead circumstances day by day, as he renews his
raiment day by day. But to us, in our lapsed estate,
resting, not advancing, resisting, not coöperating with
the divine expansion, this growth comes by shocks.

We cannot part with our friends. We cannot let
our angels go. We do not see that they only go out
that archangels may come in. We are idolaters of the
old. We do not believe in the riches of the soul, in its
proper eternity and omnipresence. We do not believe
there is any force in to-day to rival or recreate that
beautiful yesterday. We linger in the ruins of the old
tent where once we had bread and shelter and organs,
nor believe that the spirit can feed, cover, and nerve

us again. We cannot again find aught so dear, so
sweet, so graceful. But we sit and weep in vain.
The voice of the Almighty saith, "Up and onward
for ever more!" We cannot stay amid the ruins.
Neither will we rely on the new; and so we walk ever
with reverted eyes, like those monsters who look
backwards.

And yet the compensations of calamity are made
apparent to the understanding also, after long intervals of time. A fever, a mutilation, a cruel disappoint-
ment, a loss of wealth, a loss of friends, seems at the
moment unpaid loss, and unpayable. But the sure
years reveal the deep remedial force that underlies
all facts. The death of a dear friend, wife, brother,
lover, which seemed nothing but privation, somewhat
later assumes the aspect of a guide or genius; for it
commonly operates revolutions in our way of life, ter-
minates an epoch of infancy or of youth which was
waiting to be closed, breaks up a wonted occupation,
or a household, or style of living, and allows the formation of new ones more friendly to the growth of
character. It permits or constrains the formation of
new acquaintances and the reception of new influences
that prove of the first importance to the next years;
and the man or woman who would have remained a
sunny garden-flower, with no room for its roots and
too much sunshine for its head, by the falling of the
walls and the neglect of the gardener is made the
banian of the forest, yielding shade and fruit to wide
neighbourhoods of men.

ROBERT LOUIS STEVENSON

CRABBED AGE AND YOUTH

"You know my mother now and then argues very notably; always very warmly at least. I happen often to differ from her; and we both think so well of our own arguments, that we very seldom are so happy as to convince one another. A pretty common case, I believe, in all *vehement* debatings. She says, I am *too witty;* Anglice, *too pert;* I, that she is *too wise;* that is to say, being likewise put into English, *not so young as she has been.*"
— Miss Howe to Miss Harlowe, *Clarissa*, vol. II, Letter XIII.[1]

THERE is a strong feeling in favour of cowardly and prudential proverbs. The sentiments of a man while he is full of ardour and hope are to be received, it is supposed, with some qualification. But when the same person has ignominiously failed and begins to eat up his words, he should be listened to like an oracle. Most of our pocket wisdom is conceived for the use of mediocre people, to discourage them from ambitious attempts and generally console them in their mediocrity. And since mediocre people constitute the bulk of humanity, this is no doubt very properly so. But it does not follow that the one sort of proposition is any less true than the other, or that Icarus [2] is not to be more praised, and perhaps more envied, than Mr. Samuel Budgett, the Successful Merchant. The one is dead, to be sure, while the other is still in his counting-house counting out his money; and doubtless this is a consideration. But we have, on the other hand, some bold and magnanimous sayings common to high races and natures, which set forth the advantage of the losing side, and proclaim it better to be a dead lion than a living dog. It is difficult to fancy how the mediocrities reconcile such sayings with their proverbs. According to the latter, every lad who goes to sea is an egregious ass; never to forget your umbrella through a long life would seem a higher and wiser flight of achievement than to go smiling to the stake; and so long as you are a bit of a coward and inflexible in money matters, you fulfil the whole duty of man.

It is a still more difficult consideration for our average men, that while all their teachers, from Solomon down to Benjamin Franklin and the ungodly Binney, have inculcated the same ideal of manners, caution, and respectability, those characters in history who have most notoriously flown in the face of such precepts are spoken of in hyperbolical terms of praise, and honoured with public monuments in the streets of our commercial centres. This is very bewildering to the moral sense. You have Joan of Arc, who left a humble but honest and reputable livelihood under the eyes of her parents, to go a-colonelling, in the company of rowdy soldiers, against the enemies of France; surely a melancholy example for one's daughters! And then you have Columbus, who may have pioneered America, but, when all is said, was a most imprudent navigator. His life is not the kind of thing one would like to put into the hands of young people; rather, one would do one's utmost to keep it from their knowledge, as a red flag of adventure and disintegrating influence in life. The time would fail me if I were to recite all the big names in history whose exploits are perfectly irrational and even shocking to the business mind. The incongruity is speaking; and I imagine it must engender among the mediocrities a very peculiar attitude towards the nobler and showier sides of national life. They will read of the Charge of Balaclava [3] in much the same spirit as they assist at a performance of the *Lyons Mail*. Persons of substance take in the *Times* and sit composedly in pit or boxes according to the degree of their prosperity in business. As for the generals who go galloping up and down among bomb-shells in absurd cocked hats — as for the actors who raddle their faces and demean themselves for hire upon the stage — they must belong, thank God! to a different order of beings, whom we watch as we watch the clouds careering in the windy, bottomless inane or read about like characters in ancient and rather fabulous annais. Our offspring would no more think of copying their behaviour, let us hope, than of doffing their clothes and painting themselves blue in consequence of certain admissions in the first chapter of their school history of England.

Discredited as they are in practice, the cowardly proverbs hold their own in theory; and it is another instance of the same spirit, that the opinions of old men about life have been accepted as final. All sorts of allowances are made for the illusions of youth; and none, or almost none, for the disenchantments of age. It is held to be a good taunt, and somehow or other to clinch the question logically, when an old gentleman waggles his head and says: "Ah, so I thought when I was your age." It is not thought an answer at all, if the young man retorts: "My venerable sir, so I shall most probably think when I am yours." And yet the one is as good as the other, pass for pass, tit for tat, a Roland for an Oliver.

"Opinion in good men," says Milton, "is but
knowledge in the making." All opinions, properly
so called, are stages on the road to truth. It does not
follow that a man will travel any further; but if he
has really considered the world and drawn a conclusion, he has travelled as far. This does not apply
to formulæ got by rote, which are stages on the road
to nowhere but second childhood and the grave.
To have a catchword in your mouth is not the same
thing as to hold an opinion; still less is it the same
thing as to have made one for yourself. There are
too many of these catchwords in the world for people
to rap out upon you like an oath and by way of an
argument. They have a currency as intellectual
counters; and many respectable persons pay their
way with nothing else. They seem to stand for
vague bodies of theory in the background. The
imputed argument of folios full of knockdown arguments is supposed to reside in them, just as some of
the majesty of the British Empire dwells in the con-
stable's truncheon. They are used in pure superstition, as old clodhoppers spoil Latin by way of an
exorcism. And yet they are vastly serviceable
for checking unprofitable discussion and stopping the
mouths of babes and sucklings. And when a young
man comes to a certain stage of intellectual growth,
the examination of these counters forms a gymnastic
at once amusing and fortifying to the mind.

Because I have reached Paris, I am not ashamed
of having passed through Newhaven and Dieppe.
They were very good places to pass through, and I
am none the less at my destination. All my old opinions were only stages on the way to the one I now hold,
as itself is only a stage on the way to something else.

I am no more abashed at having been a red-hot
Socialist with a panacea of my own than at having
been a sucking infant. Doubtless the world is quite
right in a million ways; but you have to be kicked
about a little to convince you of the fact. And in the
meanwhile you must do something, be something,
believe something. It is not possible to keep the
mind in a state of accurate balance and blank;
and even if you could do so, instead of coming ulti-
mately to the right conclusion, you would be very
apt to remain in a state of balance and blank to per-
petuity. Even in quite intermediate stages, a dash
of enthusiasm is not a thing to be ashamed of in the
retrospect: if St. Paul had not been a very zealous
Pharisee, he would have been a colder Christian.
For my part, I look back to the time when I was
a Socialist with something like regret. I have convinced myself (for the moment) that we had better
leave these great changes to what we call blind forces;
their blindness being so much more perspicacious than
the little, peering, partial eyesight of men. I seem
to see that my own scheme would not answer; and
all the other schemes I ever heard propounded would
depress some elements of goodness just as much as
they encouraged others. Now I know that in thus
turning Conservative with years, I am going through
the normal cycle of change and travelling in the common orbit of men's opinions. I submit to this, as I
would submit to gout or grey hair, as a concomitant
of growing age or else of failing animal heat; but I
do not acknowledge that it is necessarily a change
for the better — I daresay it is deplorably for the
worse. I have no choice in the business, and can
no more resist this tendency of my mind than I

could prevent my body from beginning to totter
and decay. If I am spared (as the phrase runs) I
shall doubtless outlive some troublesome desires;
but I am in no hurry about that; nor, when the
time comes, shall I plume myself on the immunity.
Just in the same way, I do not greatly pride myself
on having outlived my belief in the fairy tales of
Socialism. Old people have faults of their own; they
tend to become cowardly, niggardly, and suspicious.
Whether from the growth of experience or the decline
of animal heat, I see that age leads to these and certain
other faults; and it follows, of course, that while in
one sense I hope I am journeying towards the truth,
in another I am indubitably posting towards these
forms and sources of error.

As we go catching and catching at this or that corner of knowledge, now getting a foresight of generous
possibilities, now chilled with a glimpse of prudence,
we may compare the headlong course of our years
to a swift torrent in which a man is carried away;
now he is dashed against a boulder, now he grapples
for a moment to a trailing spray; at the end, he is
hurled out and overwhelmed in a dark and bottomless ocean. We have no more than glimpses and
touches; we are torn away from our theories; we are
spun round and round and shown this or the other
view of life, until only fools and knaves can hold to
their opinions. We take a sight at a condition in
life, and say we have studied it; our most elaborate
view is no more than an impression. If we had
breathing space, we should take the occasion to
modify and adjust; but at this breakneck hurry, we
are no sooner boys than we are adult, no sooner in
love than married or jilted, no sooner one age than

we begin to be another, and no sooner in the fulness
of our manhood than we begin to decline towards the
grave. It is in vain to seek for consistency or expect
clear and stable views in a medium so perturbed
and fleeting. This is no cabinet science, in which
things are tested to a scruple; we theorize with
a pistol to our head; we are confronted with a new
set of conditions on which we have not only to pass
judgment, but to take action, before the hour is at
an end. And we cannot even regard ourselves as a
constant; in this flux of things, our identity itself
seems in a perpetual variation; and not infrequently
we find our own disguise the strangest in the mas-
querade. In the course of time, we grow to love things
we hated and hate things we loved. Milton is not so
dull as he once was, nor perhaps Ainsworth [4] so
amusing. It is decidedly harder to climb trees, and
not nearly so hard to keep still. There is no use
pretending; even the thrice royal game of hide and
seek has somehow lost in zest. All our attributes
are modified or changed; and it will be a poor account
of us if our views do not modify and change in a
proportion. To hold the same views at forty as we
held at twenty is to have been stupefied for a score
of years, and take rank, not as a prophet, but as an
unteachable brat, well birched and none the wiser.
It is as if a ship captain should sail to India from
the Port of London; and having brought a chart of
the Thames on deck at his first setting out, should
obstinately use no other for the whole voyage.

And mark you, it would be no less foolish to begin
at Gravesend with a chart of the Red Sea. *Si
Jeunesse savait, si Vieillesse pouvait,*[5] is a very pretty
sentiment, but not necessarily right. In five cases

out of ten, it is not so much that the young people
do not know as that they do not choose. There is
something irreverent in the speculation, but perhaps
the want of power has more to do with the wise reso-
lutions of age than we are always willing to admit.
It would be an instructive experiment to make an old
man young again and leave him all his *savoir*.   I
scarcely think he would put his money in the Sav-
ings Bank after all; I doubt if he would be such an
admirable son as we are led to expect; and as for
his conduct in love, I firmly believe he would out-
Herod Herod and put the whole of his new compeers
to the blush.   Prudence is a wooden Juggernaut, before whom Benjamin Franklin walks with the portly
air of a high priest, and after whom dances many a
successful merchant in the character of Atys.   If
a man lives to any considerable age, it cannot be
denied that he laments his imprudence, but I notice
he often laments his youth a deal more bitterly and
with a more genuine intonation.

It is customary to say that age should be considered,
because it comes last. It seems just as much to the
point, that youth comes first. And the scale fairly
kicks the beam, if you go on to add that age, in a ma-
jority of cases, never comes at all. Disease and accident make short work of even the most prosperous
persons; death costs nothing, and the expense of a
head-stone is an inconsiderable trifle to the happy heir.
To be suddenly snuffed out in the middle of ambitious
schemes, is tragical enough at best; but when a man
has been grudging himself his own life in the meanwhile, and saving up everything for the festival
that was never to be, it becomes that hysterically
loving sort of tragedy which lies on the confines of

farce. The victim is dead — and he has cunningly overreached himself: a combination of calamities none the less absurd for being grim. To husband a favourite claret until the batch turns sour, is not at all an artful stroke of policy; and how much more with a whole cellar — a whole bodily existence! People may lay down their lives with cheerfulness in the sure expectation of a blessed immortality; but that is a different affair from giving up youth with all its admirable pleasures, in the hope of a better quality of gruel in a more than problematical, nay, more than improbable, old age. We should not compliment a hungry man, who would refuse a whole dinner and reserve all his appetite for the dessert before he knew whether there was to be any dessert or not. If there be such a thing as imprudence in the world, we surely have it here. We sail in leaky bottoms and on great and perilous waters; and to take a cue from the dolorous old naval ballad, we have heard the mermaidens singing, and know that we shall never see dry land any more. Old and young, we are all on our last cruise. If there is a fill of tobacco among the crew, for God's sake pass it round, and let us have a pipe before we go!

Indeed, by the report of our elders, this nervous preparation for old age is only trouble thrown away. We fall on guard, and after all it is a friend who comes to meet us. After the sun is down and the west faded, the heavens begin to fill with shining stars. So, as we grow old, a sort of equable jog-trot of feeling is substituted for the violent ups and downs of passion and disgust; the same influence that restrains our hopes, quiets our apprehensions; if the pleasures are less intense, the troubles are milder

and more tolerable; and in a word, this period for
which we are asked to hoard up everything as for a
time of famine, is, in its own right, the richest,
easiest, and happiest of life. Nay, by managing its
own work and following its own happy inspiration,
youth is doing the best it can to endow the leisure of
age. A full, busy youth is your only prelude to a
self-contained and independent age; and the muff in-
evitably develops into the bore. There are not many
Dr. Johnsons, to set forth upon their first romantic
voyage at sixty-four. If we wish to scale Mont
Blanc or visit a thieves' kitchen in the East End, to
go down in a diving dress or up in a balloon, we must
be about it while we are still young. It will not do to
delay until we are clogged with prudence and limp-
ing with rheumatism, and people begin to ask us
"What does Gravity out of bed?" Youth is the
time to go flashing from one end of the world to the
other both in mind and body; to try the manners
of different nations; to hear the chimes at midnight;
to see sunrise in town and country; to be converted
at a revival; to circumnavigate the metaphysics,
write halting verses, run a mile to see a fire, and wait
all day long in the theatre to applaud *Hernani*.[6]
There is some meaning in the old theory about wild
oats; and a man who has not had his green-sickness
and got done with it for good, is as little to be de-
pended on as an unvaccinated infant. "It is extraordinary," says Lord Beaconsfield, one of the bright-
est and best preserved of youths up to the date of his
last novel, "it is extraordinary how hourly and how
violently change the feelings of an inexperienced
young man." And this mobility is a special talent
entrusted to his care; a sort of indestructible virginity;

a magic armour, with which he can pass unhurt
through great dangers and come unbedaubed out of
the miriest passages. Let him voyage, speculate, see
all that he can, do all that he may; his soul has as
many lives as a cat; he will live in all weathers, and
never be a halfpenny the worse. Those who go to
the devil in youth, with anything like a fair chance,
were probably little worth saving from the first;
they must have been feeble fellow-creatures made
of putty and packthread, without steel or fire, anger
or true joyfulness, in their composition; we may
sympathize with their parents, but there is not much
cause to go into mourning for themselves; for to
be quite honest, the weak brother is the worst of
mankind.

When the old man waggles his head and says,
"Ah, so I thought when I was your age," he has
proved the youth's case. Doubtless, whether from
growth of experience or decline of animal heat, he
thinks so no longer; but he thought so while he was
young; and all men have thought so while they were
young, since there was dew in the morning or haw-
thorn in May; and here is another young man add-
ing his vote to those of previous generations and rivet-
ing another link to the chain of testimony. It is as
natural and as right for a young man to be imprudent
and exaggerated, to live in swoops and circles, and
beat about his cage like any other wild thing newly
captured, as it is for old men to turn grey, or mothers
to love their offspring, or heroes to die for something
worthier than their lives.

By way of an apologue for the aged, when they
feel more than usually tempted to offer their advice,
let me recommend the following little tale. A

child who had been remarkably fond of toys (and
in particular of lead soldiers) found himself growing to
the level of acknowledged boyhood without any
abatement of this childish taste. He was thirteen;
already he had been taunted for dallying overlong
about the playbox; he had to blush if he was found
among his lead soldiers; the shades of the prison-house
were closing about him with a vengeance. There
is nothing more difficult than to put the thoughts
of children into the language of their elders; but this
is the effect of his meditations at this juncture:
"Plainly," he said, "I must give up my playthings,
in the meanwhile, since I am not in a position to
secure myself against idle jeers. At the same time,
I am sure that playthings are the very pick of life;
all people give them up out of the same pusillanimous
respect for those who are a little older; and if they
do not return to them as soon as they can, it is only
because they grow stupid and forget. I shall be wiser;
I shall conform for a while to the ways of their foolish
world; but so soon as I have made enough money,
I shall retire and shut myself up among my playthings
until the day I die." Nay, as he was passing in the
train along the Esterel mountains between Cannes and
Frejus, he remarked a pretty house in an orange garden at the angle of a bay, and decided that this should
be his Happy Valley. Astrea Redux; childhood was
to come again! The idea has an air of simple nobility
to me, not unworthy of Cincinnatus. And yet, as
the reader has probably anticipated, it is never likely
to be carried into effect. There was a worm i' the
bud, a fatal error in the premises. Childhood must
pass away, and then youth, as surely as age approaches.
The true wisdom is to be always seasonable, and to

change with good grace in changing circumstances. To love playthings as well as a child, to lead an adventurous and honourable youth, and to settle, when the time arrives, into a green and smiling age, is to be a good artist in life and deserve well of yourself and your neighbour.

You need repent none of your youthful vagaries. They may have been over the score on one side, just as those of age are probably over the score on the other. But they had a point; they not only befitted your age and expressed its attitude and passions, but they had a relation to what was outside of you, and implied criticisms on the existing state of things, which you need not allow to have been undeserved, because you now see that they were partial. All error, not merely verbal, is a strong way of stating that the current truth is incomplete. The follies of youth have a basis in sound reason, just as much as the embarrassing questions put by babes and sucklings. Their most antisocial acts indicate the defects of our society. When the torrent sweeps the man against a boulder, you must expect him to scream, and you need not be surprised if the scream is sometimes a theory. Shelley, chafing at the Church of England, discovered the cure of all evils in universal atheism. Generous lads irritated at the injustices of society, see nothing for it but the abolishment of everything and Kingdom Come of anarchy. Shelley was a young fool; so are these cocksparrow revolutionaries. But it is better to be a fool than to be dead. It is better to emit a scream in the shape of a theory than to be entirely insensible to the jars and incongruities of life and take everything as it comes in a forlorn stupidity. Some people swallow

the universe like a pill; they travel on through the
world, like smiling images pushed from behind. For
God's sake give me the young man who has brains
enough to make a fool of himself! As for the others,
the irony of facts shall take it out of their hands, and
make fools of them in downright earnest, ere the farce
be over. There shall be such a mopping and a mowing
at the last day, and such blushing and confusion of
countenance for all those who have been wise in
their own esteem, and have not learnt the rough
lessons that youth hands on to age. If we are indeed
here to perfect and complete our own natures, and
grow larger, stronger, and more sympathetic against
some noble career in the future, we had all best
bestir ourselves to the utmost while we have the time.
To equip a dull respectable person with wings would
be but to make a parody of an angel.

In short, if youth is not quite right in its opinions,
there is a strong probability that age is not much more
so. Undying hope is co-ruler of the human bosom
with infallible credulity. A man finds he has been
wrong at every preceding stage of his career, only to
deduce the astonishing conclusion that he is at last
entirely right. Mankind, after centuries of failure,
are still upon the eve of a thoroughly constitutional
millennium. Since we have explored the maze so
long without result, it follows, for poor human reason, that we cannot have to explore much longer;
close by must be the centre, with a champagne lunch-
eon and a piece of ornamental water. How if
there were no centre at all, but just one alley after
another, and the whole world a labyrinth without
end or issue?

I overheard the other day a scrap of conversation

which I take the liberty to reproduce. "What I advance is true," said one. "But not the whole truth," answered the other. "Sir," returned the first (and it seemed to me there was a smack of Dr. Johnson in the speech), "Sir, there is no such thing as the whole truth!" Indeed there is nothing so evident in life as that there are two sides to a question. History is one long illustration. The forces of nature are engaged, day by day, in cudgelling it into our backward intelligences. We never pause for a moment's consideration, but we admit it as an axiom. An enthusiast sways humanity exactly by disregarding this great truth, and dinning it into our ears that this or that question has only one possible solution; and your enthusiast is a fine florid fellow, dominates things for a while and shakes the world out of a doze; but when once he is gone, an army of quiet and uninfluential people set to work to remind us of the other side and demolish the generous imposture. While Calvin [7] is putting everybody exactly right in his *Institutes*, and hotheaded Knox [8] is thundering in the pulpit, Montaigne is already looking at the other side in his library in Perigord, and predicting that they will find as much to quarrel about in the Bible as they had found already in the Church. Age may have one side, but assuredly Youth has the other. There is nothing more certain than that both are right, except perhaps that both are wrong. Let them agree to differ; for who knows but what agreeing to differ may not be a form of agreement rather than a form of difference?

I suppose it is written that any one who sets up for a bit of a philosopher, must contradict himself to his very face. For here have I fairly talked myself into thinking that we have the whole thing before us at last; that there is no answer to the mystery, except that there are as many as you please, that there is no centre to the maze because, like the famous sphere, its centre is everywhere; and that agreeing to differ with every ceremony of politeness, is the only "one undisturbed song of pure concent" to which we are ever likely to lend our musical voices.

ARTHUR CHRISTOPHER BENSON

BOOKS

THE one room in my College which I always enter with a certain sense of desolation and sadness is the College library. There used to be a story in my days at Cambridge of a book-collecting Don who was fond of discoursing in public of the various crosses he had to bear. He was lamenting one day in Hall the unwieldly size of his library. "I really don't know what to do with my books," he said, and looked round for sympathy. "Why not read them?" said a brisk and caustic Fellow opposite. It may be thought that I am in need of the same advice, but it is not the case. There are, indeed, many books in our library; but most of them, as D. G. Rossetti used to say in his childhood of his father's learned volumes, are "no good for reading." The books of the College library are delightful, indeed, to look at; rows upon rows of big irregular volumes, with tarnished tooling and faded gilding on the sun-scorched backs. What are they? — old editions of classics, old volumes of controversial divinity, folios of the Fathers, topographical treatises, cumbrous philosophers, pamphlets from which, like dry ashes, the heat of the fire that warmed them once has fled. Take one down; it is an agreeable sight enough; there is a gentle scent of antiquity; the bumpy page crackles faintly; the big irregular print meets the eye with a pleasant and leisurely mellowness. But

what do they tell one? Very little, alas! that one
need know, very much which it would be a positive
mistake to believe. That is the worst of erudition
— that the next scholar sucks the few drops of honey
that you have accumulated, sets right your blunders,
and you are superseded. You have handed on the
torch, perhaps, and even trimmed it. Your errors,
your patient explanations, were a necessary step in
the progress of knowledge; but even now the proces-
sion has turned the corner, and is out of sight.

Yet even here, it pleases me to think, some mute
and unsuspected treasure may lurk unknown. In
a room like this, for over a couple of centuries stood
on one of the shelves an old rudely bound volume of
blank paper, the pages covered with a curious strag-
gling cipher; no one paid any heed to it, no one tried
to spell its secrets. But the day came when a Fellow
who was both inquisitive and leisurely took up
the old volume, and formed a resolve to decipher it.
Through many baffling delays, through many patient
windings, he carried his purpose out; and the result
was a celebrated Day-book, which cast much light
upon the social conditions of a past age, as well as revealed one of the most simple and genial personalities
that ever marched blithely through the pages of a
Diary.

But, even in these days of cheap print and nasty
paper, with a central library into which pours the
annual cataract of literature, these little ancient
libraries have no use left, save as repositories or store-
rooms. They belong to the days when books were
few and expensive; when few persons could acquire
a library of their own; when lecturers accumulated
knowledge that was not the property of the world;

when notes were laboriously copied and handed on
when one of the joys of learning was the consciousness of possessing secrets not known to other men.
An ancient Dean of Christ Church is said to have
given three reasons for the study of Greek; the first
was that it enabled you to read the words of the
Saviour in the original tongue; the second, that it
gave you a proper contempt for those who were ignorant of it; and the third was that it led to situations
of emolument. What a rich aroma hangs about this
judgment! The first reason is probably erroneous, the
second is un-Christian, and the third is a gross motive
which would equally apply to any professional training whatsoever.

Well, the knowledge of Greek, except for the
schoolmaster and the clergyman, has not now the
same obvious commercial value. Knowledge is
more diffused, more accessible. It is no longer
thought to be a secret, precious, rather terrible possession; the possessor is no longer venerated and
revered; on the contrary, a learned man is rather
considered likely to be tiresome. Old folios have,
indeed, become merely the stock-in-trade of the
illustrators of sensational novels. Who does not
know the absurd old man, with white silky hair,
velvet skullcap, the venerable appearance, who sits
reading a folio at an oak table, and who turns out
to be the villain of the piece, a mine of secret and un-
successful wickedness? But no one in real life reads
a folio now, because anything that is worth reprinting,
as well as a good deal that is not, is reprinted in convenient form, if not in England, at least in Germany.

And the result of it is that these College libraries
are almost wholly unvisited. It seems a pity, but

it also seems inevitable. I wish that some use could be devised for them, for these old books make at all events a very dignified and pleasant background, and the fragrance of well-warmed old leather is a delicate thing. But they are not even good places for working in, now that one has one's own books and one's own reading-chair. Moreover, if they were kept up to date, which would in itself be an expensive thing, there would come in the eternal difficulty of where to put the old books, which no one would have the heart to destroy.

Perhaps the best thing for a library like this would be not to attempt to buy books, but to subscribe like a club to a circulating library, and to let a certain number of new volumes flow through the place and lie upon the tables for a time. But, on the other hand, here in the University there seems to be little time for general reading; and indeed it is a great problem, as life goes on, as duties grow more defined, and as one becomes more and more conscious of the shortness of life, what the duty of a cultivated and open-minded man is with regard to general reading. I am inclined to think that as one grows older one may read less; it is impossible to keep up with the vast output of literature, and it is hard enough to find time to follow even the one or two branches in which one is specially interested. Almost the only books which, I think, it is a duty to read, are the lives of great contemporaries; one gets thus to have an idea of what is going on in the world, and to realize it from different points of view. New fiction, new poetry, new travels are very hard to peruse diligently. The effort, I confess, of beginning a new novel, of making acquaintance with an unfamiliar scene, of

getting the individualities of a fresh group of people
into one's head, is becoming every year harder for me;
but there are still one or two authors of fiction for
whom I have a predilection, and whose works I look
out for.   New poetry demands an even greater
effort; and as to travels, they are written so much
in the journalistic style, and consist so much of the
meals our traveller obtains at wayside stations, of
conversations with obviously reticent and even un-
intelligent persons; they have so many photogravures
of places that are exactly like other places, and of
complacent people in grotesque costumes, like supers
in a play, that one feels the whole thing to be hopelessly superficial and unreal.   Imagine a journalistic
foreigner visiting the University, lunching at the
station refreshment-room, hurrying to half-a-dozen
of the best known colleges, driving in a tram through
the main thoroughfares, looking on at a football
match, interviewing a Town Councillor, and being
presented to the Vice-Chancellor — what would
be the profit of such a record as he could give us?
What would he have seen of the quiet daily life, the
interests, the home-current of the place? The only
books of travel worth reading are those where a
person has settled deliberately in an unknown place,
really lived the life of the people, and penetrated the
secret of the landscape and the buildings.

I wish very much that there was a really good literary paper, with an editor of catholic tastes, and half-
a-dozen stimulating specialists on the staff, whose
duty would be to read the books that came out,
each in his own line, write reviews of appreciation
and not of contemptuous fault-finding, let feeble
books alone, and make it their business to tell ordi-

nary people what to read, not saving them the trouble
of reading the books that are worth reading, but spar-
ing them the task of glancing at a good many books
that are not worth reading.   Literary papers, as a
rule, either review a book with hopeless rapidity,
or tend to lag behind too much.   It would be of the
essence of such a paper as I have described, that
there should be no delay about telling one what to
look out for, and at the same time that the reviews
should be deliberate and careful.

But I think as one grows older one may take out
a license, so to speak, to read less.   One may go
back to the old restful books, where one knows
the characters well, hear the old remarks, survey the
same scenes.   One may meditate more upon one's
stores, stroll about more, just looking at life, seeing
the quiet things that are happening, and beaming
through one's spectacles.   One ought to have amassed,
as life goes on and the shadows lengthen, a good deal
of material for reflection.   And after all, reading is not
in itself a virtue; it is only one way of passing the
time; talking is another way, watching things another.
Bacon says that reading makes a full man; well, I
cannot help thinking that many people are full to the
brim when they reach the age of forty, and that much
which they afterwards put into the overcharged vase
merely drips and slobbers uncomfortably down the
side and foot.

The thing to determine then, as one's brain hardens
or softens, is what the object of reading is.   It is not,
I venture to think, what used to be called the pursuit of knowledge.   Of course, if a man is a professional teacher or a professional writer, he must read
for professional purposes, just as a coral insect must

eat to enable it to secrete the substances out of which it builds its branching house. But I am not here speaking of professional studies, but of general reading. I suppose that there are three motives for reading — the first, purely pleasureable; the second, intellectual; the third, what may be called ethical. As to the first, a man who reads at all, reads just as he eats, sleeps, and takes exercise, because he likes it; and that is probably the best reason that can be given for the practice. It is an innocent mode of passing the time, it takes one out of oneself, it is amusing. Of course, it can be carried to an excess; and a man may become a mere book-eater, as a man may become an opium-eater. I used at one time to go and stay with an old friend, a clergyman in a remote part of England. He was a bachelor and fairly well off. He did not care about exercise or his garden, and he had no taste for general society. He subscribed to the London Library and to a lending library in the little town where he lived, and he bought, too, a good many books. He must have spent, I used to calculate, about ten hours of the twenty-four in reading. He seemed to me to have read everything, old and new books alike, and he had an astonishing memory; anything that he put into his mind remained there exactly as fresh and clear as when he laid it away, so that he never needed to read a book twice. If he had lived at a University he would have been a useful man; if one wanted to know what books to read in any line, one had only to pick his brains. He could give one a list of authorities on almost every subject. But in his country parish he was entirely thrown away. He had not the least desire to make anything of his stores, or to write. He had not the

art of expression, and he was a distinctly tiresome
talker. His idea of conversation was to ask you if
you had read a number of modern novels. If he found
one that you had not read, he sketched the plot in an
intolerably prolix manner, so that it was practically
impossible to fix the mind on what he was saying.
He seemed to have no preferences in literature whatsoever; his one desire was to read everything that
came out, and his only idea of a holiday was to
go up to London and get lists of books from a bookseller. That is of course, an extreme case; and I
cannot help feeling that he would have been nearly
as usefully employed if he had confined himself to
counting the number of words in the books he read.
But, after all, he was interested and amused, and a
perfectly contented man.

As to the intellectual motive for reading, it hardly
needs discussing; the object is to get clear conceptions, to arrive at a critical sense of what is good in
literature, to have a knowledge of events and ten-
dencies of thought, to take a just view of history and
of great personalities; not to be at the mercy of theo-
rists, but to be able to correct a faulty bias by having
a large and wide view of the progress of events and
the development of thought. One who reads from
this point of view will generally find some particular
line which he intends to follow, some special region
of the mind where he is desirous to know all that can
be known; but he will, at the same time, wish to
acquaint himself in a general way with other depart-
ments of thought, so that he may be interested in
subjects in which he is not wholly well-informed,
and be able to listen, even to ask intelligent questions, in matters with which he has no minute ac-

quaintance. Such a man, if he steers clear of the contempt for indefinite views which is often the curse of men with clear and definite minds, makes the best kind of talker, stimulating and suggestive; his talk seems to open doors into gardens and corridors of the house of thought; and others, whose knowledge is fragmentary, would like to be at home, too, in that pleasant palace. But it is of the essence of such talk that it should be natural and attractive, not professional or didactic. People who are not used to Universities tend to believe that academical persons are invariably formidable. They think of them as possessed of vast stores of precise knowledge, and actuated by a merciless desire to detect and ridicule deficiencies of attainment among unprofessional people. Of course, there are people of this type to be found at a University, just as in all other professions it is possible to find uncharitable specialists who despise persons of hazy and leisurely views. But my own impression is that it is a rare type among University Dons; I think that it is far commoner at the University to meet men of great attainments combined with sincere humility and charity, for the simple reason that the most erudite specialist at a University becomes aware both of the wide diversity of knowledge and of his own limitations as well.

Personally, direct bookish talk is my abomination. A knowledge of books ought to give a man a delicate allusiveness, an aptitude for pointed quotation. A book ought to be only incidentally, not anatomically, discussed; and I am pleased to be able to think that there is a good deal of this allusive talk at the University, and that the only reason there is not more is that professional demands are so insistent, and work so thorough, that academical persons cannot keep up their general reading as they would like to do.

And when we come to what I have called, for want of a better word, the ethical motive for reading; it might sound at first as if I meant that people ought to read improving books, but that' is exactly what I do not mean. I have very strong opinions on this point, and hold that what I call the ethical motive for reading is the best of all — indeed the only true one. And yet I find a great difficulty in putting into words what is a very elusive and delicate thought. But my belief is this. As I make my slow pilgrimage through the world, a certain sense of beautiful mystery seems to gather and grow. I see that many people find the world dreary — and, indeed, there must be spaces of dreariness in it for us all, — some find it interesting; some surprising; some find it entirely satisfactory. But those who find it satisfactory seem to me, as a rule, to be tough, coarse, healthy natures, who find success attractive and food digestible; who do not trouble their heads very much about other people, but go cheerfully and optimistically on their way, closing their eyes as far as possible to things painful and sorrowful, and getting all the pleasure they can out of material enjoyments.

Well, to speak very sincerely and humbly, such a life seems to me the worst kind of failure. It is the life that men were living in the days of Noah, and out of such lives comes nothing that is wise or useful or good. Such men leave the world as they found it, except for the fact that they have eaten a little way into it, like a mite into a cheese, and leave a track of decomposition behind them.

I do not know why so much that is hard and painful

and sad is interwoven with our life here; but I see, or seem to see, that it is meant to be so interwoven. All the best and most beautiful flowers of character and thought seem to me to spring up in the track of suffering; and what is the most sorrowful of all mysteries, the mystery of death, the ceasing to be, the relinquishing of our hopes and dreams, the breaking of our dearest ties, becomes more solemn and awe-inspiring the nearer we advance to it.

I do not mean that we are to go and search for unhappiness; but, on the other hand, the only happiness worth seeking for is a happiness which takes all these dark things into account, looks them in the face, reads the secret of their dim eyes and set lips, dwells with them, and learns to be tranquil in their presence.

In this mood — and it is a mood which no thoughtful man can hope or ought to wish to escape — reading becomes less and less a searching for instructive and impressive facts, and more and more a quest after wisdom and truth and emotion. More and more I feel the impenetrability of the mystery that surrounds us; the phenomena of nature, the discoveries of science, instead of raising the veil, seem only to make the problem more complex, more bizzarre, more insoluble; the investigation of the laws of light, of electricity, of chemical action, of the causes of disease, the influence of heredity — all these things may minister to our convenience and our health, but they make the mind of God, the nature of the First Cause, an infinitely more mysterious and inconceivable problem.

But there still remains, inside, so to speak, of these astonishing facts, a whole range of intimate personal phenomena, of emotion, of relationship, or mental or spiritual conceptions, such as beauty, affection, righteousness, which seem to be an even nearer concern, even more vital to our happiness than the vast laws of which it is possible for men to be so unconscious, that centuries have rolled past without their being investigated.

And thus in such a mood reading becomes a patient tracing out of human emotion, human feeling, when confronted with the sorrows, the hopes, the motives, the sufferings which beckon us and threaten us on every side. One desires to know what pure and wise and high-hearted natures have made of the problem; one desires to let the sense of beauty — that most spiritual of all pleasures — sink deeper into the heart; one desires to share the thoughts and hopes, the dreams and visions, in the strength of which the human spirit has risen superior to suffering and death.

And thus, as I say, the reading that is done in such a mood has little of precise acquisition or definite attainment about it; it is a desire rather to feed and console the spirit — to enter the region in which it seems better to wonder than to know, to aspire rather than to define, to hope rather than to be satisfied. A spirit which walks expectantly along this path grows to learn that the secret of such happiness as we can attain lies in simplicity and courage, in sincerity and loving-kindness; it grows more and more averse to material ambitions and mean aims; it more and more desires silence and recollection and contemplation. In this mood the words of the wise fall like the tolling of sweet, grave bells upon the soul, the dreams of poets come like music heard at evening from the depth of some enchanted forest, wafted

over a wide water; we know not what instrument it is
whence the music wells, by what fingers swept, by
what lips blown; but we know that there is some
presence there that is sorrowful or glad, who has
power to translate his dream into the concord of sweet
sounds. Such a mood need not withdraw us from
life, from toil, from kindly relationships, from deep
affections; but it will rather send us back to life with
a renewed and joyful zest, with a desire to discern the
true quality of beautiful things, of fair thoughts, of
courageous hopes, of wise designs. It will make us
tolerant and forgiving, patient with stubbornness
and prejudice, simple in conduct, sincere in word,
gentle in deed; with pity for weakness, with affection for the lonely and the desolate, with admiration
for all that is noble and serene and strong.

Those who read in such a spirit will tend to resort
more and more to large and wise and beautiful books,
to press the sweetness out of old familiar thoughts,
to look more for warmth and loftiness of feeling than
for elaborate and artful expression. They will value
more and more books that speak to the soul, rather
than books that appeal to the ear and to the mind.
They will realize that it is through wisdom and force
and nobility that books retain their hold upon the
hearts of men, and not by briskness and colour and
epigram. A mind thus stored may have little grasp
of facts, little garniture of paradox and jest; but it
will be full of compassion and hope, of gentleness and
joy. . . .

Well, this thought has taken me a long way from the
College library, where the old books look somewhat
pathetically from the shelves, like aged dogs wondering why no one takes them for a walk. Monuments

of pathetic labour, tasks patiently fulfilled through
slow hours! But yet I am sure that a great deal of
joy went to the making of them, the joy of the old
scholar who settled down soberly among his papers,
and heard the silvery bell above him tell out the dear
hours that, perhaps, he would have delayed if he
could. Yes, the old books are a tender-hearted and a
joyful company; the day slips past, the sunlight
moves round the court, and steals warmly for an
hour or two into the deserted room. Life — delightful life — spins merrily past; the perennial stream of
youth flows on; and perhaps the best that the old
books can do for us is to bid us cast back a wistful
and loving thought into the past — a little gift of
love for the old labourers who wrote so diligently
in the forgotten hours, till the weary, failing hand
laid down the familiar pen, and soon lay silent in
the dust.

SAMUEL McCHORD CROTHERS

THE EVOLUTION OF THE GENTLEMAN

"What is your favorite character, Gentle Reader?"
"I like to read about gentlemen," he answers;
"it's a taste I have inherited, and I find it growing
upon me."

And yet it is not easy to define a gentleman, as
the multitudes who have made the attempt can testify.
It is one of the cases in which the dictionary does not
help one. Perhaps, after all, definitions are to be
looked upon as luxuries, not as necessities. When
Alice told her name to Humpty Dumpty, that intolerable pedant asked,—

" 'What does it mean?'

" 'Must a name mean something?' Alice asked
doubtfully.

" 'Of course it must,' Humpty Dumpty said with
a short laugh. 'My name means the shape I am, —
and a good handsome shape it is, too.'"

I suppose that almost any man, if he were asked
what a gentleman is, would answer with Humpty
Dumpty, "It is the shape I am." I judge this because, though the average man would not feel insulted
if you were to say, "You are no saint," it would not
be safe to say, "You are no gentleman."

And yet the average man has his misgivings. For
all his confident talk, he is very humble minded.
The astral body of the gentleman that he is endeavor-
ing to project at his neighbors is not sufficiently ma-
terialized for his own imperfect vision. The word

"gentleman" represents an ideal. Above whatever coarseness and sordidness there may be in actual life, there rises the ideal of a finer kind of man, with gentler manners and truer speech and braver action.

In every age we shall find the true gentleman — that is, the man who represents the best ideal of his own time, and we shall find the mimicry of him the would-be gentleman who copies the form while ignorant of the substance. These two characters furnish the material, on the one hand for the romancer, and on the other for the satirist. If there had been no real gentlemen, the epics, the solemn tragedies, and the stirring tales of chivalry would have remained unwritten; and if there had been no pretended gentlemen, the humorist would have lost many a pleasure. Always the contrasted characters are on the stage together; simple dignity is followed by strutting pomposity, and after the hero the braggart swaggers and storms. So ridicule and admiration bear rule by turns.

The idea of the gentleman involves the sense of personal dignity and worth. He is not a means to an end; he is an end in itself. How early this sense arose we may not know. Professor Huxley made merry over the sentimentalists who picture the simple dignity of primitive man. He had no admiration to throw away on "the dignified and unclothed savage sitting in solitary meditation under trees." And yet I am inclined to think that the gentleman must have appeared even before the advent of tailors. The peasants who followed Wat Tyler [1] sang, —

> "When Adam delved and Eve span
> Who was then the gentleman?"

But a writer in the age of Queen Elizabeth published a book in which he argued that Adam himself was a perfect gentleman. He had the advantage dear to the theological mind, that though affirmative proof might be lacking, it was equally difficult to prove the negative.

As civilization advances and literature catches its changing features, the outlines of the gentleman grow distinct.

In the Book of Genesis we see Abraham sitting at his tent door. Three strangers appear. When he sees them, he goes to meet them, and bows, and says to the foremost, "My Lord, if now I have found favour in thy sight, pass not away, I pray thee, from thy servant. Let a little water, I pray you, be fetched, and wash your feet, and rest yourselves under the tree: and I will fetch a morsel of bread, and comfort ye your hearts; after that ye shall pass on."

There may have been giants in those days, and churls, and all manner of barbarians, but as we watch the strangers resting under the oak we say, "There were also gentlemen in those days." How simple it all is! It is like a single palm tree outlined against the desert and the sky.

We turn to the *Analects* of Confucius and we see the Chinese gentleman. Everything with him is exact. The disciples of Confucius are careful to tell us how he adjusted the skirts of his robe before and behind, how he insisted that his mince-meat should be cut quite small and should have exactly the right proportion of rice, and that his mat must be laid straight before he would sit on it. Such details of deportment were thought very important. But we forget the

mats and the mince-meat when we read: "Three
things the master had not, — he had no prejudices,
he had no obstinacy, he had no egotism."

And we forget the fantastic garb and the stiff
Chinese genuflections, and come to the conclusion
that the true gentleman is as simple-hearted amid
the etiquette of the court as in the tent in the desert,
when we hear the master saying: "Sincerity is the
way of Heaven; the wise are the unassuming. It
is said of Virtue that over her embroidered robe she
puts a plain single garment."

When we wish to see a masculine virtue which has
no need of an embroidered garment we go to Plutarch's [2] portrait gallery of antique gentlemen. What
a breed of men they were! They were no holiday
gentlemen. With the same lofty dignity they faced
life and death. How superior they were to their fortunes. No wonder that men who had learned to
conquer themselves conquered the world.

Most of Plutarch's worthies were gentlemen,
though there were exceptions. There was, for example, Cato the Censor, who bullied the Roman
youth into virtue, and got a statue erected to
himself as the restorer of the good old manners.
Poor Plutarch, who likes to do well by his heroes, is
put to his wits' end to know what to do with testy,
patriotic, honest, fearless, parsimonious Cato. Cato
was undoubtedly a great man and a good citizen;
but when we are told how he sold his old slaves, at
a bargain, and how he left his war-horse in Spain
to save the cost of transportation, Plutarch adds,
"Whether such things be an evidence of greatness
or littleness of soul let the reader judge for himself."
The judicious reader will conclude that it is possible

to be a great man and a reformer, and yet not be quite a gentleman.

When the Roman Empire was destroyed the antique type of gentleman perished. The very names of the tribes which destroyed him have yet terrible associations. Goths, Vandals, Huns — to the civilized man of the fifth and sixth centuries these sounded like the names of wild beasts rather than of men. You might as well have said tigers, hyenas, wolves. The end had come of a civilization that had been the slow growth of centuries.

Yet out of these fierce tribes, destroyers of the old order, a new order was to arise. Out of chaos and night a new kind of gentleman was to be evolved. The romances of the Middle Ages are variations on a single theme, the appearance of the finer type of manhood and its struggle for existence. In the palace built by the enchantment of Merlin were four zones of sculpture.

> "And in the lowest beasts are slaying men
> And in the second men are slaying beasts,
> And on the third are warriors, perfect men,
> And on the fourth are men with growing wings."

Europe was in the second stage, when men were slaying beasts and what was most brutal in humanity. If the higher manhood was to live, it must fight, and so the gentleman appears, sword in hand. Whether we are reading of Charlemagne and his paladins, or of Siegfried, or of Arthur, the story is the same. The gentleman has appeared. He has come into a waste land, —

> "Thick with wet woods and many a beast therein,
> And none or few to scare or chase the beast."

He comes amid savage anarchy where heathen hordes are "reddening the sun with smoke and earth with blood." The gentleman sends forth his clear defiance. All this shall no longer be. He is ready to meet force with force; he is ready to stake his life upon the issue, the hazard of new fortunes for the race.

It is as a pioneer of the new civilization that the gentleman has pitched

> "His tent beside the forest. And he drave
> The heathen, and he slew the beast, and felled
> The forest, and let in the sun."

The ballads and romances chronicle a struggle desperate in its beginning and triumphant in its conclusion. They are in praise of force, but it is a noble force. There is something better, they say, than brute force: it is manly force. The giant is no match for the gentleman.

If we would get at the mediæval idea of the gentleman, we must not listen merely to the romances as they are retold by men ol genius in our own day. Scott and Tennyson clothe their characters in the old draperies, but their ideals are those of the nineteenth century rather than of the Middle Ages. Tennyson expressly disclaims the attempt to reproduce the King Arthur —

> "whose name, a ghost,
> Streams like a cloud, man-shaped, from mountain peak,
> And cleaves to cairn and cromlech still; or him
> Of Geoffrey's book, or him of Malleor's, one
> Touched by the adulterous finger of a time
> That hovered between war and wantonness."

When we go back and read Sir Thomas Malory's *Morte Darthur*,[3] we find ourselves among men of somewhat different mould from the knights of Tennyson's idylls. It is not the blameless King Arthur, but the passionate Sir Launcelot, who wins admiration. We hear Sir Ector crying over Launcelot's body, "Ah, Launcelot, thou wert the head of the Christian knights. Thou wert the courtliest knight that ever bare shield; and thou wert the truest friend to thy lover that ever bestrode horse; and thou wert the truest lover for a sinful man that ever loved woman; and thou wert the kindest man that ever strake with sword; and thou wert the goodliest person that ever came among press of knights; and thou wert the meekest man and the gentlest that ever ate in hall with ladies; and thou wert the sternest knight to thy mortal foe that ever put spear in the rest."

We must take, not one of these qualities, but all of them together, to understand the gentleman of those ages when good and evil struggled so fiercely for the mastery. No saint was this Sir Launcelot. There was in him no fine balance of virtues, but only a wild tumult of the blood. He was proud, self-willed, passionate, pleasure-loving; capable of great sin and of sublime expiation. What shall we say of this gentlest, sternest, kindest, goodliest, sinfulest of knights, — this man who knew no middle path, but who, when treading in perilous places and following false lights, yet draws all men admiringly to himself?

We can only say this: he was the prototype of those mighty men who were the makers of the modern world. They were the men who fought with Charlemagne, and with William the Conqueror, and with Richard; they were the men who "beat down the heathen, and upheld the Christ;" they were the men from whom came the crusades, and the feudal system, and the great charter. As we read the history, we say at one moment, "These men were mail-clad ruffians," and at the next, "What great-hearted gentlemen!"

Perhaps the wisest thing would be to confess to both judgments at once. In this stage of his evolution the gentleman may boast of feats that would now be rehearsed only in bar-rooms. This indicates that the standard of society has improved, and that what was possible once for the nobler sort of men is now characteristic of the baser sort. The modern rowdy frequently appears in the cast-off manners of the old-time gentleman. Time, the old-clothes man, thus furnishes his customers with many strange misfits. What is of importance is that through these transition years there was a ceaseless struggle to preserve the finer types of manhood.

The ideal of the mediæval gentleman was expressed in the word "gallantry." The essence of gallantry is courage; but it is not the sober courage of the stoic. It is courage charged with qualities that give it sparkle and effervescence. It is the courage that not only faces danger, but delights in it. What suggestions of physical and mental elasticity are in Shakespeare's description of the "springing, brave Plantagenet!" Scott's lines express the gallant spirit: —

> "One crowded hour of glorious life
> Is worth an age without a name."

Gallantry came to have another implication, equally characteristic. The knight was gallant not only in war, but in love also. There had come a new worship,

the worship of woman.   In the Church it found expression in the adoration of the Madonna, but in the
camp and court it found its place as well.   Chivalry
was the elaborate and often fantastic ritual, and the
gentleman was minister at the altar.   The ancient
gentleman stood alone; the mediæval gentleman
offered all to the lady of his love.   Here, too, gallantry
implied the same overflowing joy in life.   If you are
anxious to find a test by which to recognize the time
when you are growing old, — so old that imagination is chilled within you, — I should advise you to
turn to the chapter in the Romance of King Arthur
entitled "How Queen Guenever went maying with
certain Knights of the Table Round, clad all in
green."   Then read: "So it befell in the month
of May, Queen Guenever called unto her knights
and she gave them warning that early upon the mor-
row she would ride maying into the woods and fields
besides Westminster, and I warn you that none of
you but that he be well horsed and that ye all be
clothed in green. . . . I shall bring with me ten
ladies and every knight shall have a squire and two
yeomen.   So upon the morn they took their horses
with the Queen and rode on maying through the
woods and meadows in great joy and delights."

If you cannot see them riding on, a gallant company
over the meadows, and if you hear no echoes of their
laughter, and if there is no longer any enchantment in the vision of that time when all were "blithe
and debonair," then undoubtedly you are growing
old.   It is time to close the romances: perhaps you
may still find solace in Young's "Night Thoughts" [4]
or Pollok's "Course of Time." [5]   Happy are they
who far into the seventies still see Queen Guenever

riding in the pleasant month of May: these are they who have found the true fountain of youth.

The gentleman militant will always be the hero of ballads and romances; and in spite of the apostles of realism, I fancy he has not lost his charm. There are Jeremiahs of evolution, who tell us that after a time men will be so highly developed as to have neither hair nor teeth. In that day, when the operating dentists have ceased from troubling, and given way to the manufacturing dentists, and the barbers have been superseded by the wig-makers, it is quite possible that the romances may give place to some tedious department of comparative mythology. In that day, Chaucer's knight who "loved chevalrie, trouthe and honour, fredom and curtesie," will be forgotten, though his armor on the museum walls will be learnedly described. But that dreadful day is still far distant; before it comes, not only teeth and hair must be improved out of existence, but a substitute must be found for good red blood. Till that time "no laggard in love or dastard in war," can steal our hearts from young Lochinvar.

The sixteenth century marks an epoch in the history of the gentleman, as in all else. Old ideas disappear, to come again in new combinations. Familiar words take on meanings that completely transform them. The same hands wielded the sword and the pen. The scholars, the artists, the poets, began to feel a sense of personal worth, and carried the gallant spirit of the gentleman into their work. They were not mere specialists, but men of action. The artist was not only an instrument to give pleasure to others, but he was himself a centre of admiration. Out of his new consciousness how many interesting characters were produced! There were men who engaged in controversies as if they were tournaments, and who wrote books and painted pictures and carved statues, not in the spirit of professionalism, but as those who would in this activity enjoy "one crowded hour of glorious life." Very frequently these gentlemen and scholars, and gentlemen and artists, overdid the matter, and were more belligerent in disposition than were the warriors with whom they began to claim equality.

To this self-assertion we owe the most delightful of autobiographies, — that of Benvenuto Cellini.[6] He aspired to be not only an artist, but a fine gentleman. No one could be more certain of the sufficiency of Humpty Dumpty's definition of a gentleman than was he.

If we did not have his word for it, we could scarcely believe that any one could be so valiant in fight and so uninterrupted in the pursuit of honor without its interfering with his professional work. Take, for example, that memorable day when, escaping from the magistrates, he makes an attack upon the household of his enemy, Gherado Guascanti. "I found them at table; and Gherado, who had been the cause of the quarrel, flung himself upon me. I stabbed him in the breast, piercing doublet and jerkin, but doing him not the least harm in the world." After this attack, and after magnanimously pardoning Gherado's father, mother, and sisters, he says: "I ran storming down the staircase, and when I reached the street I found all the rest of the household, more than twelve persons: one of them seized an iron shovel, another a thick iron pipe; one had an anvil, some hammers, some cudgels. When I got among them, raging like a mad bull, I flung four or five to the earth, and fell down with them myself, continually aiming my dagger now at one, and now at another. Those who remained upright plied with both hands with all their force, giving it me with hammers, cudgels, and the anvil; but inasmuch as God does sometimes mercifully intervene, he so ordered that neither they nor I did harm to one another."

What fine old days those were, when the toughness of skin matched so wonderfully the stoutness of heart! One has a suspicion that in these degenerate times, were a family dinner-party interrupted by such an avalanche of daggers, cudgels, and anvils, some one would be hurt. As for Benvenuto, he does not so much as complain of a headache.

There is an easy, gentleman-like grace in the way in which he recounts his incidental homicides. When he is hiding behind a hedge at midnight, waiting for the opportunity to assassinate his enemies, his heart is open to all the sweet influences of nature, and he enjoys "the glorious heaven of stars." He was not only an artist and a fine gentleman, but a saint as well, and "often had recourse with pious heart to holy prayers." Above all, he had the indubitable evidence of sainthood, a halo. "I will not omit to relate another circumstance, which is perhaps the most remarkable that ever happened to any one. I do so in order to justify the divinity of God and of his secrets, who deigned to grant me this great favor: forever since the time of my strange vision until now, an aureole of glory (marvelous to relate) has rested on my head. This is visible to every sort of man to whom I have chosen to point it out, but these have been few." He adds ingenuously, "I am always

able to see it." He says, "I first became aware of
it in France, at Paris; for the air in those parts is so
much freer from mists that one can see it far better
than in Italy."

Happy Benvenuto with his Parisian halo, which did
not interfere with the many arts of self-defense! His
self-complacency was possible only in a stage of evolution when the saint and the assassin were not
altogether clearly differentiated. Some one has said,
"Give me the luxuries of life, and I can get along
without the necessities." Like many of his time,
Benvenuto had all the luxuries that belong to the
character of a Christian gentleman, though he was
destitute of the necessities. An appreciation of common honesty as an essential to a gentleman seems
to be more slowly developed than the more romantic
sentiment that is called honor.

The evolution of the gentleman has its main line
of progress where there is a constant but slow advance;
but, on the other hand, there are arrested developments, and quaint survivals, and abortive attempts.

In each generation there have been men of fashion
who have mistaken themselves for gentlemen. They
are uninteresting enough while in the flesh, but after
a generation or two they become very quaint and
curious, when considered as specimens. Each generation imagines that it has discovered a new variety,
and invents a name for it. The dude, the swell, the
dandy, the fop, the spark, the macaroni, the blade,
the popinjay, the coxcomb, — these are butterflies
of endless summers. There is here endless variation,
but no advancement. One fashion comes after
another, but we cannot call it better. One would
like to see representatives of the different generations

in full dress. What variety in oaths and small talk! What anachronisms in swords and canes and eye-glasses, in ruffles, in collars, in wigs! What affluence in powders and perfumes and colors! But "will they know each other there?" The real gentlemen would be sure to recognize each other. Abraham and Marcus Aurelius and Confucius would find much in common. Launcelot and Sir Phillip Sidney and Chinese Gordon would need no introduction. Montaigne and Mr. Spectator and the Autocrat of the Breakfast Table would fall into delightful chat. But would a "swell" recognize a "spark"? And might we not expect a "dude" to fall into immoderate laughter at the sight of a "popinjay"?

Fashion has its revenges. Nothing seems so ridiculous to it as an old fashion. The fop has no toleration for the obsolete foppery. The artificial gentleman is as inconceivable out of his artificial surroundings as the waxen-faced gentleman of the clothing store outside his show window.

There was Beau Nash,[7] for example, — a much-admired person in his day, when he ruled from his throne in the pump-room at Bath. Everything was in keeping. There was Queen Anne architecture, and Queen Anne furniture, and Queen Anne religion, and the Queen Anne fashion in fine gentlemen. What a curious piece of bricabrac this fine gentleman was, to be sure! He was not fitted for any useful purpose under the sun, but in his place he was quite ornamental, and undoubtedly very expensive. Art was as self-complacent as if nature had never been invented. What multitudes of the baser sort must be employed in furnishing the fine gentleman with clothes! All Bath admired the way in which Beau Nash refused to pay for them. Once when a vulgar tradesman insisted on payment, Nash compromised by lending him twenty pounds, — which he did with the air of a prince. So great was the impression he made upon his time that a statue was erected to him, while beneath were placed the busts of two minor contemporaries, Pope and Newton. This led Lord Chesterfield[8] to write: —

> "This statue placed the busts between
> Adds to the satire strength,
> Wisdom and wit are little seen,
> But folly at full length."

Lord Chesterfield himself had nothing in common with the absurd imitation gentleman, and yet the gentleman whom he described and pretended to admire was altogether artificial. He was the Machiavelli of the fashionable world. He saw through it, and recognized its hollowness; but such as it was it must be accepted. The only thing was to learn how to get on in it. "In courts you may expect to meet connections without friendships, enmities without hatred, appearances saved and realities sacrificed, good manners and bad morals."

There is something earnestly didactic about Lord Chesterfield. He gives line upon line, and precept upon precept, to his "dear boy." Never did a Puritan father teach more conscientiously the shorter catechism than did he the whole duty of the gentleman, which was to save appearances even though he must sacrifice reality. "My dear boy," he writes affectionately, "I advise you to trust neither man nor woman more than is absolutely necessary. Accept proffered friendships with great civility, but with great incredulity."

No youth was more strenuously prodded up the steep and narrow path of virtue than was little Philip Stanhope up the steep and narrow path of fashion. Worldliness made into a religion was not without its asceticism. "Though you think you dance well, do not think you dance well enough. Though you are told that you are genteel, still aim at being genteeler. . . . Airs, address, manners, graces, are of such infinite importance and are so essentially necessary to you that now, as the time of meeting draws near, I tremble for fear that I may not find you possessed of them."

Lord Chesterfield's gentleman was a man of the world; but it was, after all, a very hard and empty world. It was a world that had no eternal laws, only changing fashions. It had no broken hearts, only broken vows. It was a world covered with glittering ice, and the gentleman was one who had learned to skim over its dangerous places, not caring what happened to those who followed him.

It is a relief to get away from such a world, and, leaving the fine gentleman behind, to take the rumbling stagecoach to the estates of Sir Roger de Coverley. His is not the great world at all, and his interests are limited to his own parish. But it is a real world, and much better suited to a real gentleman. His fashions are not the fashions of the court, but they are the fashions that wear. Even when following the hounds Sir Roger has time for friendly greetings. "The farmers' sons thought themselves happy if they could open a gate for the good old knight, which he requited with a nod or a smile, and a kind inquiry after their fathers and uncles."

But even dear old Roger de Coverley [9] cannot rest

undisturbed as an ideal gentleman. He belonged,
after all, to a privileged order, and there is a force
at work to destroy all social privileges. A generation
of farmers' sons must arise not to be so easily satisfied with a kindly nod and smile. Liberty, fraternity,
and equality have to be reckoned with. Democracy
has come with its levelling processes.

> "The calm Olympian height
> Of ancient order feels its bases yield."

In a revolutionary period the virtues of an aristocracy become more irritating than their vices. People
cease to attribute merit to what comes through good
fortune. No wonder that the disciples of the older
time cry: —

> "What hope for the fine-nerved humanities
> That made earth gracious once with gentler arts?"

What becomes of the gentleman in an age of demo-
cratic equality? Just what becomes of every ideal
when the time for its fulfillment has come. It is freed
from its limitations and enters into a larger life.

Let us remember that the gentleman was always
a lover of equality, and of the graces that can only
grow in the society of equals. The gentleman of an
aristocracy is at his best only when he is among
his peers. There is a little circle within which there
is no pushing, no assumption of superiority. Each
member seeks not his own, but finds pleasure in a
gracious interchange of services.

But an aristocracy leaves only a restricted sphere
for such good manners. Outside the group to which
he belongs the gentleman is compelled by imperious
custom to play the part of a superior being. It has

always been distasteful and humiliating to him. It is only an essentially vulgar nature that can really be pleased with the servility of others.

An ideal democracy is a society in which good manners are universal. There is no arrogance and no cringing, but social intercourse is based on mutual respect. This ideal democracy has not been perfected, but the type of men who are creating it has already been evolved. Among all the crude and sordid elements of modern life, we see the stirring of a new chivalry. It is based on the recognition of the worth and dignity of the common man.

Milton in memorable words points out the transition which must take place from the gentleman of romance to the gentleman of enduring reality. After narrating how, in his youth, he betook himself "to those lofty fables and romances which recount in solemn cantos the deeds of knighthood founded by our victorious kings and thence had in renown through all Christendom," he says: "This my mind gave me that every free and gentle spirit, without that oath ought to be born a knight, nor needed to expect a gilt spur or the laying on of a sword upon his shoulder."

AGNES REPPLIER

THE MISSION OF HUMOUR

"Laughter is my object: 'tis a property
In man, essential to his reason."

AMERICAN humour is the pride of American hearts.
It is held to be our splendid national characteristic,
which we flaunt in the faces of other nations, con-
ceiving them to have been less favoured by Providence. Just as the most effective way to disparage
an author or an acquaintance — and we have often
occasion to disparage both — is to say that he lacks
a sense of humour, so the most effective criticism we
can pass upon a nation is to deny this valuable quality. American critics have written the most charming things about the keenness of American speech,
the breadth and insight of American drollery, the
electric current in American veins; and we, reading
these pleasant felicitations, are wont to thank God
with greater fervour than the occasion demands
that we are more merry and wise than our neighbours.
Mr. Brander Matthews, for example, has told us
that there are newspaper writers in New York who
have cultivated a wit, "not unlike Voltaire's."
He mistrusts this wit because he finds it "corroding
and disintegrating;" but he makes the comparison
with that casual assurance which is a feature of
American criticism.

Indeed, our delight in our own humour has tempted
us to over-rate both its literary value and its correc-

tive qualities. We are never so apt to lose our sense of proportion as when we consider those beloved writers whom we hold to be humourists because they have made us laugh. It may be conceded that, as a people, we have an abiding and somewhat disquieting sense of fun. We are nimble of speech, we are more prone to levity than to seriousness, we are able to recognize a vital truth when it is presented to us under the familiar aspect of a jest, and we habitually allow ourselves certain forms of exaggeration, accepting, perhaps unconsciously, Hazlitt's verdict: "Lying is a species of wit, and shows spirit and invention." It is true also that no adequate provision is made in this country for the defective but valuable class without humour, which in England is exceedingly well cared for. American letters, American journalism, and American speech are so coloured by pleasantries, so accentuated by ridicule, that the silent and stodgy men, who are apt to represent a nation's real strength, hardly know where to turn for a little saving dulness. A deep vein of irony runs through every grade of society, making it possible for us to laugh at our own bitter discomfiture, and to scoff with startling distinctness at the evils which we passively permit. Just as the French monarchy under Louis the Fourteenth was wittily defined as despotism tempered by epigram, so the United States have been described as a free republic fettered by jokes, and the taunt conveys a half-truth which it is worth our while to consider.

Now there are many who affirm that the humourist's point of view is, on the whole, the fairest from which the world can be judged. It is equally remote from the misleading side-lights of the pessimist and from the wilful blindness of the optimist. It sees things with uncompromising clearness, but it judges of them with tolerance and good temper. Moreover, a sense of the ridiculous is a sound preservative of social virtues. It places a proper emphasis on the judgments of our associates, it saves us from pitfalls of vanity and self-assurance, it lays the basis of that propriety and decorum of conduct upon which is founded the charm of intercourse among equals. And what it does for us individually, it does for us collectively. Our national apprehension of a jest fosters whatever grace of modesty we have to show. We dare not inflate ourselves as superbly as we should like to do, because our genial countrymen stand ever ready to prick us into sudden collapse. "It is the laugh we enjoy at our own expense which betrays us to the rest of the world."

Perhaps we laugh too readily. Perhaps we are sometimes amused when we ought to be angry. Perhaps we jest when it is our plain duty to reform. Here lies the danger of our national light-mindedness, — for it is seldom light-heartedness; we are no whit more light-hearted than our neighbours. A carping English critic has declared that American humour consists in speaking of hideous things with levity; and while so harsh a charge is necessarily unjust, it makes clear one abiding difference between the nations. An Englishman never laughs — except officially in "Punch" — over any form of political degradation. He is not in the least amused by jobbery, by bad service, by broken pledges. The seamy side of civilized life is not to him a subject for sympathetic mirth. He can pity the stupidity which does not perceive that it is cheated and betrayed; but

penetration allied to indifference awakens his wondering contempt.   "If you think it amusing to be
imposed on," an Englishwoman once said to me,
"you need never be at a loss for a joke."

In good truth, we know what a man is like by the
things he finds laughable, we gauge both his understanding and his culture by his sense of the becoming and of the absurd. If the capacity for laughter be one of the things which separates men from
brutes, the quality of laughter draws a sharp divid-
ing-line between the trained intelligence and the
vacant mind.   The humour of a race interprets
the character of a race, and the mental condition of
which laughter is the expression is something which it
behooves the student of human nature and the student of national traits to understand very clearly.

Now our American humour is, on the whole, good-
tempered and decent.   It is scandalously irreverent
(reverence is a quality which seems to have been left
out of our composition); but it has neither the pitiless-
ness of the Latin, nor the grossness of the Teuton
jest. As Mr. Gilbert said of Sir Beerbohm Tree's
"Hamlet," it is funny without being coarse. We
have at our best the quality of being amusing in an
agreeable, almost an amiable, fashion; but then we
have also the rare good fortune to be very easily
amused.   Think of the current jokes provided for
our entertainment week by week, and day by day.
Think of the comic supplement of our Sunday newspapers, designed for the refreshment of the feeble-
minded, and calculated to blight the spirits of any
ordinarily intelligent household.   Think of the de-
bilitated jests and stories which a time-honoured
custom inserts at the back of some of our magazines

It seems to be the custom of happy American parents to report to editors the infantile prattle of their engaging little children, and the editors print it for the benefit of those who escape the infliction first-hand. There is a story, pleasant but piteous, of Voltaire's listening with what patience he could muster to a comedy which was being interpreted by its author. At a certain point the dramatist read, "At this the Chevalier laughed;" whereupon Voltaire murmured enviously, "How fortunate the Chevalier was!" I think of that story whenever I am struck afresh by the ease with which we are moved to mirth.

A painstaking German student, who has traced the history of humour back to its earliest foundations, is of the opinion that there are eleven original jokes known to the world, or rather that there are eleven original and basic situations which have given birth to the world's jokes; and that all the pleasantries with which we are daily entertained are variations of these eleven originals, traceable directly or indirectly to the same sources. There are times when we are disposed to think eleven too generous a computation, and there are less weary moments in which the inexhaustible supply of situations still suggests fresh possibilities of laughter. Granted that the ever fertile mother-in-law jest and the one about the talkative barber were venerable in the days of Plutarch; there are others more securely and more deservedly rooted in public esteem which are, by comparison, new. Christianity, for example, must be held responsible for the missionary and cannibal joke, of which we have grown weary unto death; but which nevertheless possesses astonishing vitality, and exhibits remarkable breadth of treatment. Sydney Smith did not disdain to honour it with a joyous and unclerical quatrain; and the agreeable author of "Rab and his Friends" has told us the story of his fragile little schoolmate whose mother had destined him for a missionary, "though goodness knows there was n't enough of him to go around among so many heathen."

To Christianity is due also the somewhat ribald mirth which has clung for centuries about Saint Peter as gatekeeper of Heaven. We can trace this mirth back to the rude jests of the earliest miracle plays. We see these jests repeated over and over again in the folklore of Latin and Germanic nations. And if we open a comic journal to-day, there is more than a chance that we shall find Saint Peter, key in hand, uttering his time-honoured witticisms. This well-worn situation depends, as a rule, upon that common element of funmaking, the incongruous. Saint Peter invaded by air-ships. Saint Peter outwitting a squad of banner-flying suffragettes. Saint Peter losing his saintly temper over the expansive philanthropy of millionaires. Now and then a bit of true satire, like Mr. Kipling's "Tomlinson," conveys its deeper lesson to humanity. A recently told French story describes a lady of good reputation, family, and estate, presenting herself fearlessly at the gates of Heaven. Saint Peter receives her politely, and leads her through a street filled with lofty and beautiful mansions, any one of which she thinks will satisfy her requirements; but, to her amazement, they pass them by. Next they come to more modest but still charming houses with which she feels she could be reasonably content; but again they pass them by.

Finally they reach a small and mean dwelling in a
small and mean thoroughfare. "This," says Saint
Peter, "is your habitation." "This!" cries the indignant lady; "I could not possibly live in any place
so shabby and inadequate." "I am sorry, madame,"
replies the saint urbanely, "but we have done the
best we could with the materials you furnished us."

There are no bounds to the loyalty with which
mankind clings to a well-established jest, there is
no limit to the number of times a tale will bear re-
telling. Occasionally we give it a fresh setting, adorn
it with fresh accessories, and present it as new-born
to the world; but this is only another indication of our
affectionate tenacity. I have heard that caustic
gibe of Queen Elizabeth's anent the bishop's lady and
the bishop's wife (the Tudors had a biting wit of
their own) retold at the expense of an excellent lady,
the wife of a living American bishop; and the story of
the girl, who, professing religion, gave her ear-rings
to a sister, because she knew they were taking *her*
to Hell, — a story which dates from the early Wes-
leyan revivals in England, — I have heard located in
Philadelphia, and assigned to one of Mr. Torrey's
evangelistic services. We still resort, as in the days
of Sheridan, to our memories for our jokes, and to
our imaginations for our facts. Moreover, we Americans have jests of our own, poor things for the most
part, but our own. They are current from the
Atlantic to the Pacific, they appear with commend-
able regularity in our newspapers and comic jour-
nals, and they have become endeared to us by a lifetime of intimacy. The salient characteristics of our
great cities, the accepted traditions of our mining-
camps, the contrast between East and West, the

still more familiar contrast between the torpor of Philadelphia and Brooklyn ("in the midst of life," says Mr. Oliver Herford, "we are — in Brooklyn") and the uneasy speed of New York,— these things furnish abundant material for everyday American humour. There is, for example, the encounter between the Boston girl and the Chicago girl, who, in real life, might often be taken for each other; but who, in the American joke, are as sharply differentiated as the Esquimo and the Hottentot. And there is the little Boston boy who always wears spectacles, who is always named Waldo, and who makes some innocent remark about "Literary Ethics," or the "Conduct of Life." We have known this little boy too long to bear a parting from him. Indeed, the mere suggestion that all Bostonians are forever emersed in Emerson is one which gives unfailing delight to the receptive American mind. It is a poor community which cannot furnish its archaic jest for the diversion of its neighbours.

The finest example of our bulldog resoluteness in holding on to a comic situation, or what we conceive to be a comic situation, may be seen every year when the twenty-second of February draws near, and the shops of our great and grateful Republic break out into an irruption of little hatchets, by which curious insignia we have chosen to commemorate our first President. These toys, occasionally combined with sprigs of artificial cherries, are hailed with unflagging delight, and purchased with what appears to be patriotic fervour. I have seen letter-carriers and post-office clerks wearing little hatchets in their button-holes, as though they were party buttons, or temperance badges. It is our great national joke, which I presume gains point from the dignified and reticent character of General Washington, and from the fact that he would have been sincerely unhappy could he have foreseen the senile character of a jest, destined, through our love of absurdity, our careful cultivation of the inappropriate, to be linked forever with his name.

The easy exaggeration which is a distinctive feature of American humour, and about which so much has been said and written, has its counterpart in sober and truth-telling England, though we are always amazed when we find it there, and fall to wondering, as we never wonder at home, in what spirit it was received. There are two kinds of exaggeration; exaggeration of statement, which is a somewhat primitive form of humour, and exaggeration of phrase, which implies a dexterous misuse of language, a skilful juggling with words. Sir John Robinson gives, as an admirable instance of exaggeration of statement, the remark of an American in London that his dining-room ceiling was so low that he could not have anything for dinner but soles. Sir John thought this could have been said only by an American, only by one accustomed to have a joke swiftly catalogued as a joke, and suffered to pass. An English jester must always take into account the mental attitude which finds "Gulliver's Travels" incredible. When Mr. Edward FitzGerald said that the church at Woodbridge was so damp that fungi grew about the communion rail, Woodbridge ladies offered an indignant denial. When Dr. Thomson, the witty master of Trinity, observed of an undergraduate that "all the time he could spare from the neglect of his duties he gave to the adornment of his person," the sarcasm made its slow way into print; whereupon an intelligent British reader wrote to the periodical which had printed it, and explained painstakingly that, inasmuch as·it was not possible to spare time from the neglect of anything, the criticism was inaccurate.

Exaggeration of phrase, as well as the studied understatement which is an even more effective form of ridicule, seem natural products of American humour. They sound, wherever we hear them, familiar to our ears. It is hard to believe that an English barrister, and not a Texas ranchman, described Boston as a town where respectability stalked unchecked. Mazarin's plaintive reflection, "Nothing is so disagreeable as to be obscurely hanged," carries with it an echo of Wyoming or Arizona. Mr. Gilbert's analysis of Hamlet's mental disorder,

> "Hamlet is idiotically insane,
> With lucid intervals of lunacy,"—

has the pure flavour of American wit, — a wit which finds its most audacious expression in burlesquing bitter things, and which misfits its words with diabolic ingenuity. To match these alien jests, which sound so like our own, we have the whispered warning of an American usher (also quoted by Sir John Robinson) who opened the door to a late comer at one of Mr. Matthew Arnold's lectures: "Will you please make as little noise as you can, sir. The audience is asleep;" and the comprehensive remark of a New England scholar and wit that he never wanted to do anything in his life, that he did not find it was expensive, unwholesome, or immoral. This last observation embraces the wisdom of the centuries. Solomon would have endorsed it, and it is supremely quotable as expressing a common experience with very uncommon felicity.

When we leave the open field of exaggeration, that broad area which is our chosen territory, and seek for subtler qualities in American humour, we find here and there a witticism which, while admittedly our own, has in it an Old World quality. The epigrammatic remark of a Boston woman that men get and forget and women give and forgive, shows the fine, sharp finish of Sydney Smith or Sheridan. A Philadelphia woman's observation that she knew there could be no marriages in Heaven, because — "Well, women were there no doubt in plenty, and some men; but not a man whom any woman would have," is strikingly French. The word of a New York broker, when Mr. Roosevelt sailed for Africa, "Wall Street expects every lion to do its duty!" equals in brevity and malice the keen-edged satire of Italy. No sharper thrust was ever made at prince or potentate.

The truth is that our love of a jest knows no limit and respects no law. The incongruities of an unequal civilization (we live in the land of contrasts) have accustomed us to absurdities, and reconciled us to ridicule. We rather like being satirized by our own countrymen. We are very kind and a little cruel to our humourists. We crown them with praise, we hold them to our hearts, we pay them any price they ask for their wares; but we insist upon their being funny all the time. Once a humourist, always a humourist, is our way of thinking; and we resent even a saving lapse into seriousness on the part of those who have had the good or the ill fortune to make us laugh.

England is equally obdurate in this regard. Her

love of laughter has been consecrated by Oxford,
— Oxford, the dignified refuge of English scholar-
ship, which passed by a score of American scholars to
bestow her honours on our great American joker.
And because of this love of laughter, so desperate in
a serious nation, English jesters have enjoyed the uneasy privileges of a court fool. Look at poor Hood.
What he really loved was to wallow in the pathetic,
— to write such harrowing verses as "The Bridge of
Sighs," and the "Song of the Shirt" (which achieved
the rare distinction of being printed — like the "Beggar's Petition"— on cotton handkerchiefs), and the
"Lady's Dream." Every time he broke from his
traces, he plunged into these morasses of melancholy;
but he was always pulled out again, and reharnessed
to his jokes. He would have liked to be funny occasionally and spontaneously, and it was the will
of his master, the public, that he should be funny all
the time, or starve. Lord Chesterfield wisely said
that a man should live within his wit as well as within
his income; but if Hood had lived within his wit —
which might then have possessed a vital and lasting
quality — he would have had no income. His role
in life was like that of a dancing bear, which is held
to commit a solecism every time it settles wearily
down on the four legs nature gave it.

The same tyrannous demand hounded Mr. Eugene
Field along his joke-strewn path. Chicago, struggling
with vast and difficult problems, felt the need o
laughter, and required of Mr. Field that he shoulc
make her laugh. He accepted the responsibility, and,
as a reward, his memory is hallowed in the city he
loved and derided. New York echoes this sentiment
(New York echoes more than she proclaims; she con-

firms rather than imitates); and when Mr. Francis
Wilson wrote some years ago a charming and enthusiastic paper for the "Century Mazagine," he claimed
that Mr. Field was so great a humourist as to be
— what all great humourists are, — a moralist as well.
But he had little to quote which could be received as
evidence in a court of criticism; and many of the
paragraphs which he deemed it worth while to reprint
were melancholy instances of that jaded wit, that
exhausted vitality, which in no wise represented Mr.
Field's mirth-loving spirit, but only the things which
were ground out of him when he was not in a mirth-
ful mood.

The truth is that humour as a lucrative profession
is a purely modern device, and one which is much to
be deplored. The older humourists knew the value
of light and shade. Their fun was precious in proportion to its parsimony. The essence of humour is
that it should be unexpected, that it should embody
an element of surprise, that it should startle us out
of that reasonable gravity which, after all, must be
our habitual frame of mind. But the professional
humourist cannot afford to be unexpected. The ex-
igencies of his vocation compel him to be relentlessly
droll from his first page to his last, and this accumulated drollery weighs like lead. Compared to it,
sermons are as thistle-down, and political economy
is gay.

It is hard to estimate the value of humour as a national trait. Life has its appropriate levities, its comedy side. We cannot "see it clearly and see it whole,"
without recognizing a great many absurdities which
ought to be laughed at, a great deal of nonsense which
is a fair target for ridicule. The heaviest charge

brought against American humour is that it never
keeps its target well in view.   We laugh, but we
are not purged by laughter of our follies; we jest, but
our jests are apt to have a kitten's sportive irrespon-
sibility.   The lawyer offers a witticism in place of an
argument, the diner-out tells an amusing story in
lieu of conversation.   Even the clergyman does not
disdain a joke, heedless of Dr. Johnson's warning
which should save him from that pitfall.   Smart-
ness furnishes sufficient excuse for the impertinence of children, and with purposeless satire the
daily papers deride the highest dignitaries of the
land.

Yet while always to be reckoned with in life and
letters, American humour is not a powerful and con-
sistent factor either for destruction or for reform.
It lacks, for the most part, a logical basis, and the
dignity of a supreme aim.   Moliere's humour
amounted to a philosophy of life.   He was wont to
say that it was a difficult task to make gentlefolk
laugh; but he succeeded in making them laugh at
that which was laughable in themselves.   He aimed
his shafts at the fallacies and the duplicities which
his countrymen ardently cherished, and he scorned
the cheaper wit which contents itself with mocking
at idols already discredited.   As a result, he purged
society, not of the follies that consumed it, but of the
illusion that these follies were noble, graceful, and
wise.   "We do not plough or sow for fools," says
a Russian proverb, "they grow of themselves;"
but humour has accomplished a mighty work if it
helps us to see that a fool is a fool, and not a prophet
in the market-place.   And if the man in the market-
place chances to be a prophet, his message is safe

from assault.   No laughter can silence him, no ridicule weaken his words.

Carlyle's grim humour was also drilled into efficacy. He used it in orderly fashion; he gave it force by a stern principle of repression. He had (what wise man has not?) an honest respect for dulness, knowing that a strong and free people argues best — as Mr. Bagehot puts it — "in platoons." He had some measure of mercy for folly. But against the whole complicated business of pretence, against the pious, and respectable, and patriotic hypocrisies of a successful civilization, he hurled his taunts with such true aim that it is not too much to say there has been less real comfort and safety in lying ever since.

These are victories worth recording, and there is a big battlefield for American humour when it finds itself ready for the fray, when it leaves off firing squibs, and settles down to a compelling cannonade, when it aims less at the superficial incongruities of life, and more at the deep-rooted delusions which rob us of fair fame. It has done its best work in the field of political satire, where the "Bigelow Papers" hit hard in their day, where Nast's cartoons helped to overthrow the Tweed dynasty, and where the indolent and luminous genius of Mr. Dooley has widened our mental horizon. Mr. Dooley is a philosopher, but his is the philosophy of the looker-on, of that genuine unconcern which finds Saint George and the dragon to be both a trifle ridiculous. He is always undisturbed, always illuminating, and not infrequently amusing; but he anticipates the smiling indifference with which those who come after us will look back upon our enthusiasms and absurdities. Humour, as he sees it, is that thrice blessed quality which enables us to laugh, when otherwise we should be in danger of weeping. "We are ridiculous animals," observes Horace Walpole unsympathetically, "and if angels have any fun in their hearts, how we must divert them."

It is this clear-sighted, non-combative humour which Americans love and prize, and the absence of which they reckon a heavy loss. Nor do they always ask, "a loss to whom?" Charles Lamb said it was no misfortune for a man to have a sulky temper. It was his friends who were unfortunate. And so with the man who has no sense of humour. He gets along very well without it. He is not aware that anything is lacking. He is not mourning his lot. What loss there is, his friends and neighbours bear. A man destitute of humour is apt to be a formidable person, not subject to sudden deviations from his chosen path, and incapable of frittering away his elementary forces by pottering over both sides of a question. He is often to be respected, sometimes to be feared, and always—if possible — to be avoided. His are the qualities which distance enables us to recognize and value at their worth. He fills his place in the scheme of creation; but it is for us to see that his place is not next to ours at table, where his unresponsiveness narrows the conversational area, and dulls the contagious ardour of speech. He may add to the wisdom of the ages, but he lessens the gaiety of life.

LE BARON RUSSELL BRIGGS

THE TRANSITION FROM SCHOOL TO COLLEGE

COLLEGE life is the supreme privilege of youth. Rich men's sons from private schools may take it carelessly, as something to enjoy unearned, like their own daily bread; yet the true title to it is the title earned in college day by day. The privilege of entering college admits to the privilege of deserving college; college life belongs to the great things, at once joyous and solemn, that are not to be entered into lightly.

Now the things that are not to be entered into lightly (such as marriage and the ministry) are often the things that men enter prepared viciously or not prepared at all; and college life is no exception. "There had always lain a pleasant notion at the back of his head," says Mr. Kipling of Harvey Cheyne's father, who had left the boy to the care of a useless wife, "that some day, when he had rounded off everything and the boy had left college, he would take his son to his heart and lead him into his possessions. Then that boy, he argued, as busy fathers do, would instantly become his companion, partner, and ally; and there would follow splendid years of great works carried out together, — the old head backing the young fire." Such fatal gaps in calculation, common with preoccupied fathers, are not uncommon with teachers,— the very men whose life-work is fitting boys for life.

To prepare a boy for examinations that admit to college requires skill, but is easy; to prepare a boy for college is a problem that no teacher and no school has ever solved. In the widest sense, the transition from school to college is almost coincident with the transition from youth to manhood, — often a time when the physical being is excitable and ill controlled, when the mind suffers from the lassitude of rapid bodily growth, and when the youth's whole conception of his relation to other people is distorted by conceit. Sensitive to his own importance, just beginning to know his power for good or evil, he is shot into new and exciting surroundings, — out of a discipline that drove and held him with whip and rein into a discipline that trusts him to see the road and to travel in it. If we add to this the new and alluring arguments for vice as an expression of fully developed manhood, we have some notion of the struggle in which a boy — away from home, it may be, for the first time — is expected to conquer. The best school is the school that best prepares him for this struggle; not the school that guards him most sternly or most tenderly, nor the school that guards him not at all, but the school that steadily increases his responsibility, and as steadily strengthens him to meet it. The best college is the college that makes him a man.

The first feeling of a Freshman is confusion; the next is often a strange elation at the discovery that now at last his elders have given him his head. "I never shall forget," says a noted preacher, "how I felt when I found myself a Freshman, — a feeling that all restraint was gone, and that I might go to the Devil just as fast as I pleased." This is the transition from school to college.

In a man's life there must be, as everybody knows, a perilous time of going out into the world. To many it comes at the beginning of a college course; to many — possibly to most who go to college at all — it has already come at school. The larger and less protected boarding school or academy is constantly threatened with every vice known to a college; the cloistered private school affords, from its lack of opportunity for some vices, peculiar temptation to others; the day school, if in or near a large city, contains boys for whose bad habits, not yet revealed, their parents by and by will hold the college responsible. I remember a group of boys going daily from cultivated homes to an excellent school, each of whom, in college, came to one grief or another, and each of whom, I am convinced, had made straight at home and at school the way to that grief. The transition from school to college was merely the continuation in a larger world of what they had begun in a smaller.

A continuation is what the transition ought to be: the problem is how to make it a continuation of the right sort. "What is the matter with your college?" says a teacher who cares beyond all else for the moral and religious welfare of his pupils. "I keep my boys for years: I send them to you in September, and by Christmas half of them have degenerated. They have lost punctuality; they have lost application; they have no responsibility; and some of them are gone to the bad." "What is the matter with your school," the college retorts, "that in half a dozen years it cannot teach a boy to stand up three months? College is the world: fitting for college is fitting for life; what is the matter with your school?" He who loses his ideals loses the very bloom of life. To see a young man's ideals rapidly slipping away, while his face grows coarser and coarser, is one of the saddest sights in college or out of it. What is his training good for, if it has not taught him the folly, the misery, and the wrong of dabbling in evil? If he must believe that no man is wise till he has come to know the resorts of gamblers and harlots, and has indulged himself for experience' sake in a little gentlemanly vice, can he not put off the acquaintance four years more, by the end of which time he may have learned some wiser way of getting wisdom? Besides, in the course of those four years (and the chance is better than even) he may meet some girl for whose sake he will be glad that his record has been clean. Can-not a school which closely watches its boys while their characters are moulding teach them to keep their heads level and their hearts true, save them from the wrong that never can be righted, send them to college and through college, faulty it must be, but at least unstained?

The main object of school and college is the same, — to establish character, and to make that character more efficient through knowledge; to make moral character more efficient through mental discipline. In the transition from school to college, continuity of the best influence, mental and moral, is the thing most needful. Oddly enough, the only continuity worthy of the name is often (in its outward aspect) neither mental nor moral, but athletic. An athlete is watched at school as an athlete, enters college as an athlete; and if he is a good athlete, and if he takes decent care of his body, he continues his college course as an athlete, — with new experiences, it is true, but always with the thread of continuity fairly visible, and with the relation of training to success clearly in view. Palpably bad as the management of college athletics has been and is, misleading as the predominance of athletics in an institution of learning may be, the fact remains that in athletics lies a saving power, and that for many a boy no better bridge of the gap between school and college has yet been found. The Freshman athlete, left to himself, is likely to fall behind in his studies; but unless he is singularly unreasonable or vicious, he is where an older student of clear head and strong will can keep him straight, — can at least save him from those deplorable falls that, to a greater or less degree, bruise and taint a whole life. "The trouble will begin," said a wise man, talking to sub-Freshmen, "in the first fortnight. Some evening you will be with a lot of friends in somebody's room, when something is proposed that you know isn't just right. Stop it if you can; if not, go home and go to bed, and in the morning you will be glad you didn't stay." The first danger in the transition from boyhood to manhood is the danger in what is called "knowing life." It is so easy to let mere vulgar curiosity pose as the search for truth. A Senior who had been in a fight at a public dance said in defense of himself: "I think I have led a pretty clean life in these four years; but I believe that going among all sorts of people and knowing them is the best thing college life can give us." The old poet knew better:—

> "Let no man say there, 'Virtue's flinty wall
>   Shall lock vice in me; I'll do none but know all.'
> Men are sponges, which, to pour out, receive;
>   Who know false play, rather than lose, deceive;
> For in best understandings sin began;
>   Angels sinned first, then devils, and then man."

Here comes in to advantage the ambition of the athlete. Football begins with or before the college year. Training for football means early hours, clean life, constant occupation for body and mind. Breach of training means ostracism. That this game tides many a Freshman over a great danger, by keeping him healthily occupied, I have come firmly to believe. It supplies what President Eliot calls a "new and effective motive for resisting all sins which weaken or corrupt the body;" it appeals to ambition and to self-restraint; it gives to crude youth a task in which crude youth can attain finish and skill, can feel the power that comes of surmounting tremendous obstacles and of recognition for surmounting them; moreover, like war, it affords an outlet for the reckless courage of young manhood, — the same reckless courage that in idle days drives young men headlong into vice.

Has not hard study, also, a saving power? Yes, for some boys; but for a boy full of animal spirits, and not spurred to intellectual effort by poverty, the pressure is often too gentle, the reward too remote. Such a youth may be, in the first place, too well pleased with himself to understand his relation to his fellow men and the respectability of labor. He may fail to see that college life does not of itself make a man distinguished; in a vague way, he feels that the university is gratefully ornamented by his presence. No human creature can be more complacent than a Freshman, unless it is a Sophomore: yet the Freshman may be simply a being who, with no particular merit of his own, has received a great opportunity; and the Sophomore may be simply a being who has abused that opportunity for a year.

Now the Freshman meets, in a large modern college, a new theory of intellectual discipline. As Professor Peabody has beautifully expressed it, he passes "from the sense of study as an obligation to the sense of study as an opportunity." Too often he regards study as an inferior opportunity; and having an option between study and loafing, he takes loafing. "In the Medical School," said a first-year medical student, "they give you a lot to do; and nobody cares in the least whether you do it." In other words, the Medical School may rely on the combined stimulus of intellectual ambition and bread and butter: its Faculty need not prod or cosset; it is a place of Devil take the hindmost. Yet the change in the attitude of teacher to pupil is not more sharply marked between college and medical school than between preparatory school and college. "There are only two ways of getting work out of a *boy*," said a young college graduate. "One is through emulation; the other is to stand behind and kick him.[1] Mr. X (a well-known schoolmaster) says, 'Jones, will you please do this or that;' Mr. Y stands behind Jones and kicks him into college." I do not accept the young graduate's alternative; but I have to admit that many boys are kicked, or whipped, or cosseted, or otherwise personally conducted into college, and, once there, are as hopelessly lost as a baby turned lose in London. "It took me about two years in college to get my bearings," said an earnest man, now a superintendent of schools. "I did n't loaf; I simply did n't know how to get at things. In those days there was nobody to go to for advice; and I had never *read*

[1] Both ways are known in football, besides what is called "cursing up."

anything, — had never been inside of a public library.
I did n't know where or how to take hold."

This is the story of a man who longed to take hold;
and we must remember that many of our college boys
do not at first care whether they take hold or not.
It is only in football, not in study, that they have
learned to tackle, and to tackle low. "A bolstered
boy," says a wise mother, "is an unfortunate man."
Many of these boys have been bolstered; many are
mothers' boys; many have crammed day and night
through the hot season to get into college, and, once
in, draw a long breath and lie down. The main
object of life is attained; and for any secondary object
they are too tired to work. The old time-table of
morning school gives place to a confusing arrangement
which spreads recitations and lectures unevenly over
the different days. They walk to a large lecture room,
where a man who is not going to question them that
day talks for an hour, more or less audibly. He is a
long way off; [1] and though he is talking to somebody,
he seems not to be talking to them. It is hard to
listen; and if they take notes (a highly educational
process) the notes will be poor: besides, if they
need notes, they can buy them later. Why not let
the lecture go, and sleep, or carve the furniture, or
think about something else (girls, for instance)?
These boys are in a poor frame of mind for new
methods of instruction; yet new methods of instruction they must have. They must learn to depend
upon themselves, to become men; and they must learn
that hardest lesson of all, — that a man's freedom
consists in binding himself: still again, they must

[1] A student whose name begins with Y told me once that he had
never had a good seat in his life.

learn these things at an age when the average boy
has an ill-seasoned body, a half-trained mind, jarred
nerves, his first large sum of money, all manner of
diverting temptations, and a profound sense of his
own importance. How can they be taken down, and
not taken down too much, — thrown, and not thrown
too hard? How can they be taught the responsibility
of freedom? They face, it may be, an elective system
which, at first sight, seems to make elective, not this
or that study merely, but the habit of studying at
all. Already they have been weakened by the failure of the modern parent and the modern educator
to see steadily the power that is born of overcoming
difficulties. What the mind indolently shrinks from
is readily mistaken, by fond mothers, mercenary
tutors, and some better people, as not suited to the
genius of the boy in question. "It is too much for
Jamie to learn those stupid rules of syntax, when he
has a passion for natural history;" or, "George never
could learn geometry, — and after all, we none of
us use geometry in later life. He expects to be a
lawyer, like his father; and I can't think of any good
geometry can do him."

The change "from the sense of study as an obligation to the sense of study as an opportunity" is a noble
change for persons mature enough to turn opportunity
into obligation: it is not a noble change for those who
choose such studies only as they think they can pass
with bought notes. Knowledge that does not overcome difficulties, knowledge that merely absorbs
what it can without disagreeable effort, is not power;
it is not even manly receptivity. Milton, to be sure,
patient toiler and conqueror though he was, cried in
his pain, "God loves not to plough out the heart of

our endeavours with overhard and sad tasks;" but an
overhard and sad task may be a plain duty; and even
Milton, when he said this, was trying to get rid of
what some people would call a plain duty,— his wife.
When we consider the mass and variety of the Freshman's temptations, and what some one has called the
"strain on their higher motives," we wonder more and
more at the strength of the temptation to knowledge,
whereby so many stand steady, and work their way
out into clear-headed and trustworthy manhood.

One way to deal with these strange, excited, inexperienced, and intensely human things called Freshmen is to let them flounder till they drown or swim;
and this way has been advocated by men who have
no boys of their own. It is delightfully simple, if we
can only shut eye and ear and heart and conscience;
and it has a kind of plausibility in the examples
of men who through rough usage have achieved strong
character. "The objection," as the master of a
great school said the other day, "is the waste; and,"
he added, "it is such an awful thing to waste human
life!" This method is a cruel method, ignoring all the
sensibilities of that delicate, high-strung instrument
which we call the soul. If none but the fittest survived, the cruelty might be defended; but some, who
unhappily cannot drown, become cramped swim-
mers for all their days. Busy and worn as a college
teacher usually is, thirsty for the advancement of
learning as he is assumed always to be, he cannot
let hundreds of young men pass before him unheeded
and unfriended. At Harvard College, the Faculty,
through its system of advisers for Freshmen, has
made a beginning; and though there are hardly
enough advisers to go round, the system has proved its

usefulness. At Harvard College, also, a large com-
mittee of Seniors and Juniors has assumed some responsibility for all the Freshmen. Each undertakes
to see at the beginning of the year the Freshmen
assigned to him, and to give every one of them, besides
kindly greeting and good advice, the feeling that an
experienced undergraduate may be counted on as a
friend in need.

Whether colleges should guard their students more
closely than they do — whether, for example, they
should with gates and bars protect their dormitories
against the inroads of bad women — is an open question. For the deliberately vicious such safeguards
would amount to nothing; but for the weak they might
lessen the danger of sudden temptation. Of what
schools should do I can say little; for with schools
I have little experience: but this I know, that some
system of gradually increased responsibility is best
in theory, and has proved good in practice. The
scheme of making the older and more influential boys
"prefects" has worked well in at least one large preparatory school, and shows its excellence in the attitude of the prefects when they come to college.
This scheme makes a confident appeal to the maturity
of some boys and the reasonableness of all, trusting all
to see that the best hopes of teacher and scholar are
one and the same.

The system of gradually increased responsibility
at school must be met halfway by the system of
friendly supervision at college,— supervision in which
the older undergraduates are quite as important as
the Faculty. The Sophomore who enjoys hazing
(like the dean who employs spies) is an enemy to
civilization. The true state of mind, whether for

professor or for student, was expressed by a college teacher long ago. "I hold it," he said, "a part of my business to do what I can for any wight that comes to this place." When all students of all colleges, and all boys of all schools, believe, and have the right to believe, that their teachers are their friends; when the educated public recognizes the truth that school and college should help each other in lifting our youth to the high ground of character, — the school never forgetting that boys are to be men, and the college never forgetting that men have been boys, — we shall come to the ideal of education. Toward this ideal we are moving, slowly but steadily. When we reach it, or even come so near it as to see it always, we shall cease to dread the transition from school to college.

NOTES

MICHEL DE MONTAIGNE (Page 1)

MICHEL DE MONTAIGNE (1533–92), originator of the Essay, was born in a chateau in Perigord, France. He received an excellent classical education, engaged for some time in military service, and took a minor part in the complicated politics of his century. In March, 1571, he resolved to settle down to a period of quiet writing and meditation, and for nine years he lived as a country squire, composing his famous *Essais*. With the publication of the first edition of this book in 1580, he went on a journey to Italy, only to be recalled by his election as Mayor of Bordeaux, an office which he held for four years. Meanwhile he made important revisions of his *Essais*, the final text appearing in 1588. His death occurred in 1592.

Montaigne was a man of even temperament, tolerant nature, and active curiosity. Unassuming and simple in his tastes, he had nevertheless a profound knowledge of life and of human nature. His philosophy was a mild skepticism, depending on the theory that, as we can attain only to relative truth, we should be content to admit our ignorance of problems which reason and common sense cannot solve. In his essays he aimed primarily "to produce an accurate portrait of his own soul." They are informal and desultory, enlivened by anecdotes and quotations, and full of the frankest personal confessions. Their style is easy, vivid, and confidential. Montaigne's work, says Dowden, "is of all books the most sociable, a living companion rather than a book, playful and humorous, amiable and well bred, learned without pedantry and wise without severity." He is not only the inventor but the great master of the Familiar Essay.

Against Idleness (page 1)

The best of Montaigne's essays are too long to be included in this collection. *Against Idleness*, however, given here in the translation by Charles Cotton, is representative of the author's method: his habit of quotation, his constant use of anecdotes drawn from the classics and from contemporary history, and his easy familiar style.

1. **Vespasian:** Roman Emperor, A.D. 69–79.
2. **Adrian:** commonly called Hadrian. Roman Emperor, A.D. 117–38.
3. **One:** probably Henry IV (Henry of Navarre), King of France, 1589–1610.
4. **Soliman I:** Turkish Sultan, 1520–66.
5. **Ottoman family:** the family of the Turkish Sultans, of whom Bajazet II and Amurath III were members.
6. **Edward III:** King of England, 1327–77.
7. **Charles V:** King of France, 1364–80, who recovered from Edward III most of the English possessions in France.
8. **Julian:** Roman Emperor, A.D. 360–63.
9. **Xenophon:** an Athenian historian, B.C. 434?–355?
10. **Seneca:** a Roman Stoic philosopher, B.C. 4?–A.D. 65.
11. **Fez:** a district in Morocco in northern Africa.
12. **Cato:** Marcus Porcius Cato, leader of the Roman aristocratic party, who allied himself with Pompey and committed suicide in 46 B.C., after having been defeated by Julius Cæsar in the battle of Thapsus.

FRANCIS BACON (Page 8)

FRANCIS BACON (1561–1626) was an English statesman, author, and philosopher, who, under James I, rose steadily to be Solicitor-General (1607), Attorney-General (1613), and Lord Chancellor (1618), with the titles of Baron Verulam and Viscount St. Alban. In 1621, however, he was convicted of accepting bribes and given a heavy sentence of fine and imprisonment, which fortunately was never fully carried out. He died in 1626, as a result of a chill caught while he was testing the value of snow as a preservative of flesh.

Bacon's work in philosophy and science was, of course, his greatest achievement, earning him the title of "the father of the inductive method." For us, however, he is interesting as being the first Englishman to follow in the steps of Montaigne as an essayist. Bacon's earliest collection of ten *Essays* was published in 1597, five years after Montaigne's death. In 1612, a second edition of thirty-eight essays was printed; and in 1625, a third revision. containing fifty-eight essays, appeared. In these later volumes the author omitted, changed, and added not a little, for he was a conscientious writer, seeking earnestly for the clearest and most effective mode of expression.

The *Essays* were mainly recreatior.3 from Bacon's other studies. The first group of ten have nothing of the detailed, gossipy style of Montaigne's *Essais;* they are short and pithy, made up of compact and often unconnected observations on a topic, so that they seem to be merely a series of maxims or sententious comments. In the later essays Bacon became more discursive; but he never acquired the fullness and grace of Montaigne. The spirit of Bacon's work is worldly, prudent, and discreet, and the philosophy which he teaches is one of shrewd and undisguised expediency.

Despite their brevity, Bacon's essays are clear and direct in thought, tolerant in feeling, and penetrating in their insight into human faults and frailities. The themes treated are weighty, and nearly every line presents food for reflection. Little care is wasted on style as an end in itself. Bacon is concerned mainly with making language a key to his ideas. Autobiographical touches may be met with here and there, but never as we come across them on every page of Montaigne.

Of Travel (page 8)

1. **Allow:** approve.
2. **Consistories:** councils.
3. **Disputations:** formal debates.
4. **Card:** chart or map.
5. **Adamant:** lodestone or magnet.
6. **Country manners:** manners of his own country.
7. **Prick in:** plant.

Of Expense (page 10)

1. **Voluntary undoing:** willing poverty. Cf. Matthew xix, 24.
2. **Doubting:** fearing.
3. **Certainties:** fixed income and expenditures.
4. **As well:** as surely.

Of Youth and Age (page 12)

This essay should be compared with Stevenson's *Crabbed Age and Youth* (page 128), which deals with the same general subject.

1. **Septimius Severus:** Roman Emperor, A.D. 193–211.
2. **"Juventutem," etc.:** "He passed a youth full of errors, nay of wild excesses."
3. **Cosmus:** made Duke of Florence in 1537.
4. **Gaston de Fois:** probably the Duc de Nemours (1489–1512), nephew of Louis XII of France.
5. **Care not to:** do not hesitate to.
6. **Rabbin:** rabbi or master.
7. **Hermogenes:** a Greek rhetorician of the second century, B.C.
8. **Tully:** Marcus Tullius Cicero (B.C. 106–43), the greatest of Roman orators.
9. **Hortensius:** a well-known Roman orator (B.C. 114–50), at one time Cicero's rival.
10. **"Idem manebat," etc.:** "He remained the same, though so to remain was unbecoming."
11. **Scipio Africanus:** a famous Roman general (B.C. 234–183), who defeated Hannibal at Zama in B.C. 202.
12. **Livy:** Titus Livius (B.C. 59–A.D. 17), a great Roman historian.
13. **"Ultima," etc.:** "His last actions were not equal to his first."

Of Studies (page 14)

This essay, because of its remarkable compression of style and richness of thought, is generally considered to be Bacon's best.

1. **Privateness and retiring:** solitude and retreat.
2. **Proyning:** cultivating.
3. **Curiously:** carefully.
4. **Flashy:** insipid.
5. **Conference:** conversation.
6. **"Abeunt studia," etc.:** "Studies translate themselves into character."
7. **Stone:** a disease of the bladder or kidneys.
8. **Reins:** the kidneys.
9. **"Cymini sectores:"** "splitters of cumin-seeds;" i.e., "hair-splitters."

CHARLES LAMB (Page 16)

CHARLES LAMB (1775–1834), rightly called the best-beloved of English authors, was born in London and educated at Christ's Hospital. Obliged while still a boy to leave school in order to help in supporting his family, he secured a clerical position in the South-Sea House, and later with the East India Company, where he remained until 1825. In his spare hours he tried his hand, not unsuccessfully, at poetry and plays; but his real fame did not come until 1820, when he began contributing to the *London Magazine* a series of essays signed "Elia." Twenty-eight of these were gathered in one volume in 1823 as *Essays of Elia*, and a second collection, *Last Essays of Elia*, appeared in 1833. Lamb's delightful personality and whimsical ways made him a general favorite in a circle of prominent literary people. He died in 1834, leaving a sister, Mary, to whose care he had devoted himself for many years.

Lamb, says an appreciative critic, had every quality of intellect, — "energy, keenness, justness, precision." What lends most attractiveness to his essays, however, is his inimitable humor, combined with his exquisite pathos. He was a man of wide sympathies, of discriminating literary and artistic taste, and of deep reverence for the past: and these characteristics fill his work with charm. His style is flexible and graceful, with unexpected illuminating phrases and quaint turns of speech. In a very real sense the essays mirror the man himself, with his oddities, his curious prejudices, his old-fashioned habit of mind, and his perfect humanity. He holds properly the place among English writers that Montaigne has among the French.

A Dissertation upon Roast Pig (page 16)

This essay first appeared in the *London Magazine* for September 1822. The narrative element occupies a more conspicuous place in this than in most essays; but it is used principally for its suggestive value, and it does not mar the complete effect.

1. **My friend M.:** Thomas Manning, Lamb's life-long friend, with whom he kept up an entertaining correspondence.
2. **Confucius:** the greatest of Chinese philosophers, who lived about B.C. 550–478.
3. **Locke:** John Locke (1632–1704), the English philosopher, and author of the *Essay on Human Understanding*.
4. **Mundus edibilis:** world of eatables.
5. **Princeps obsoniorum:** prince of viands.
6. **Amor immunditiæ:** love of uncleanness.
7. The quotation is from Coleridge's *Epitaph on an Infant*.

8. **St. Omer's:** a Roman Catholic college in France, for English students. Lamb is simply assuming that he attended it.

9. **Per flagellatione extremam:** by a tremendous thrashing.

Poor Relations (page 25)

This was first printed in the *London Magazine* for May, 1823. It is a good example of the reminiscent manner which Lamb uses so frequently in his essays.

1. **Agathocles:** the son of a humble potter. He rose to the generalship of the army, and finally became ruler of all Sicily.

2. **Mordecai:** a Jew at the court of King Ahasuerus of Persia. Esther, the queen, was his adopted daughter. For the specific phrase "a Mordecai in your gate," see *Esther* iv, 1–3.

3. **Aliquando, etc.:** sometimes he had to be restrained.

4. **Richard Amlet, Esq.:** a character in *The Confederacy* (1705), the best comedy of John Vanbrugh (1672–1726), an English dramatist.

5. **Poor W——:** a reference to a friend of Lamb's, named Favell.

6. **Nessian venom:** Nessus was a centaur slain by Hercules. Nessus, before his death, told Dejanira, the wife of Hercules, that if she would steep her husband's shirt in his blood, it would preserve the love of Hercules for her. Hercules. however, was poisoned by the shirt, and died. Thus Nessus had his revenge.

7. **Hugh Latimer** (1485–1555), the famous bishop and martyr, had worn a servitor's gown at Cambridge.

8. **Richard Hooker** (1553–1600), the noted theologian, had been once a poor boy at Oxford.

9. **Artist Evangelist:** St. Luke, who, according to tradition, was a painter as well as a physician.

10. **San Sebastian,** in Spain, was besieged in 1813 by the Duke of Wellington, and finally captured.

11. **Hugo Grotius** (1583–1645) was a Dutch jurist, who founded a system of international law.

The Superannuated Man (page 34)

This essay, published in the *London Magazine* for May, 1825, gives an account, substantially accurate, of Lamb's retirement from active service in the India House, which took place on the last Tuesday of March, 1825. Lamb retired on an annual pension of four hundred and fifty pounds.

1. The line is from Virgil's *Eclogues*, I.
2. John O'Keefe (1747–1833) was an Irish playwright.
3. L——: the Lacy mentioned later.
4. B——: the Bosanquet mentioned later.
5. These are fictitious names given by Lamb to the Directors of the East India House.
6. **Esto perpetua!** "May it be perpetual!" These were the last words of Paolo Sarpi (1552–1623), the Venetian historian.
7. Old Bastille: the notorious prison in Paris, destroyed by a mob during the French Revolution.
8. The quotation is taken inaccurately from Middleton's *Mayor of Queenboro*, Act I, Scene 1.
9. The lines are from *The Vestal Virgin, or the Roman Ladies*, Act V, Scene 1, a play by Sir Robert Howard (1626–98).
10. Sir Thomas Gresham (d. 1579) founded the Royal Exchange, and other members of the same family were Lord Mayors of London.
11. Richard Whittington (d. 1423) was the famous poor boy who became Lord Mayor of London.
12. Thomas Aquinas (c. 1225–74) was a mediæval theologian.
13. Carthusian: a monk of the Carthusian order, founded in 1086 by St. Bruno, and established at Chartreuse.
14. Elgin marbles: the great collection of Greek sculptures brought to England by Lord Elgin in the early nineteenth century, and placed in the British Museum.
15. Cum dignitate: a fragment of Cicero's phrase, *otium cum dignitate*, leisure with dignity.
16. Opus, etc.: the work is accomplished.

WILLIAM HAZLITT (Page 44)

WILLIAM HAZLITT (1778–1830), the friend and contemporary rival of Lamb as an essayist, was born in Maidstone and was the son of a Unitarian clergyman. Hazlitt himself studied for the ministry, but a meeting with Coleridge in 1798 turned him from this project. For a time he hesitated between art and literature, but he gradually drifted into writing, and, after 1812, was occupied mainly with contributing to periodicals and lecturing. He quarreled with his first wife, and was divorced from her in 1822; his second wife left him shortly after their marriage. A contentious critic and untiring controversialist, Hazlitt engaged in many disputes and was subjected by his enemies to much abuse. He was a man of sincere and definite convictions, but also of violent prejudices. His temper, moreover, was so irritable and savage that even his closest friends found him sometimes difficult to deal with.

"Hazlitt is the essayist, as Shelley is the lyrist, *par excellence*," says Mr. Oliver Elton. He published in all over a hundred essays covering a wide range of thought, and nearly every one is of rare merit. In his criticisms of literature he has seldom been surpassed. His work is better represented, however, by essays of the Montaigne type on miscellaneous subjects, in which he shows himself to be a clear and cogent thinker, a fascinating commentator on art, literature, and life, and a master of a nervous and incisive style. His prose, with its effect of "living if abrupt speech," is packed with epigrams and passages of brilliant imaginative power.

Hazlitt's essays are rich in quotations which, as one writer says, "glimmer like burnished threads in the texture of his prose." In annotating the selections in this volume, it has seemed best not to devote space to pointing out the source of these quotations. They are used so naturally and effectively that they form an intrinsic part of the essays themselves, and little is to be gained by directing students to the books from which they are taken.

On Going a Journey (page 44)

This essay first appeared in the *New Monthly Magazine*, January, 1822, under the heading, "Table Talk," No. 1. From the very beginning the personal note is struck. Hazlitt chats about himself, telling of his likes and dislikes, his partialities and aversions.

1. **William Cobbett** (1762–1835) was an essayist and political writer.
2. **Laurence Sterne** (1713–68), the author of *Tristram Shandy*.
3. **C——:** Samuel Taylor Coleridge (1772–1834), the philosopher and poet, whose influence on Hazlitt was strong and enduring.
4. **L——:** Charles Lamb (see page 49), one of Hazlitt's best friends.
5. **Procul, etc.:** "stand far off, O profane souls!"
6. **Gribelin's engravings:** Simon Gribelin (1661–1733) published his engravings of Raphael's cartoons in 1707.

7. **Paul and Virginia:** a novel published in 1788 by Bernardin St. Pierre.

8. **Camilla,** a novel by Frances Burney (1752–1840), afterwards Madame D'Arblay, was published in 1796.

9. The *New Éloïse* (*La Nouvelle Héloïse*) was a novel published by Jean-Jacques Rousseau (1712–78) in 1761.

10. **Bon bouche:** tidbit.

11. **Stonehenge:** a circle of huge stones, possibly of Druid origin, lying in the midst of Salisbury Plain, a vast level district in southern England.

12. **Bodleian:** a famous library at Oxford founded by Sir Thomas Bodley.

13. **Blenheim:** the estate and castle of the Marlborough family, given to the first Duke of Marlborough by the English nation. It is some miles north of Oxford.

On a Sun-Dial (page 57)

This essay was written in Italy in 1825, and appeared in the *New Monthly Magazine* for October, 1827.

1. **Memento mori:** reminder of death.

2. These two French proverbs may be translated: "Love helps to pass away the time;" "Time makes Love pass away."

3. **In transitu:** in a course of transition.

4. **Caput mortuum:** death's-head.

5. "Come, my boy; I am more of a child than you are."

6. "We think the same of what does not appear and of what does not exist."

7. **In vacuo:** in a vacuum.

8. **The Beggars' Opera:** written by John Gay (1685–1732) and presented in 1728 with great popular success.

9. **Venice Preserved:** one of the great English tragedies. It was written by Thomas Otway (1651–85) in 1682.

On the Feeling of Immortality in Youth (page 70)

This essay, one of Hazlitt's finest, appeared in the *Monthly Magazine* for March, 1827. It should be compared with Bacon's *Youth and Age* (see page 12) and Stevenson's *Crabbed Age and Youth* (see page 128). Hazlitt here shows the noble eloquence so characteristic of his style at its best.

1. **Divinæ particula auræ:** part of divine air.

THOMAS DE QUINCEY (Page 79)

THOMAS DE QUINCEY (1785–1859), born in Manchester, England, had a solitary boyhood, given over to brooding and study. At Worcester College, Oxford, where he spent a year or two, he was known as "a strange being who associated with no one." Early in life he became a victim of the opium habit, and, although at times he seemed completely recovered, he never wholly ceased to take drugs. After 1809, when he settled in the Lake Country near Wordsworth and Coleridge, he devoted himself to a kind of higher journalism. His *Confessions of an English Opium-Eater* appeared in the *London Magazine* during 1821, contemporaneously with some of Lamb's essays. Without any very firm grasp on reality, De Quincey was given to introspection, philosophical speculation, and dreaming. Intellectually in some fields he was a mighty figure, but he dealt commonly with the intangible and vague. He possessed a marvelous style: diffuse, rambling, and sometimes incoherent, but often distinguished by gorgeous imagery and an eloquence almost Miltonic.

Much of De Quincey's work is of the "hack" variety, for he was the great contributor of his day. No one of his essays shows much power of concentration or organization. On the other hand, some of his prose is truly splendid in its roll of language and its sweep of sentence structure. In choosing an essay which will represent him at his best, it has been necessary to select a portion of a larger work. *The Vision of Sudden Death*, really a section of *The English Mail-Coach*, is absolutely complete in itself, and illustrates, even better than the more familiar *Joan of Arc*, the ornate style, the analytical method, and the rhetorical force which characterize the true De Quincey.

The Vision of Sudden Death (page 79)

1. **Jus dominii:** right of ownership.
2. **Jus gentium:** the law of nations.
3. **"Monstrum,"** etc.: from Virgil's *Æneid*, III, 658. De Quincey, in the passage following, gives a translation. The allusion is to Polyphemus, the Cyclops, whose eye was put out by Ulysses.
4. **Calendars:** three princes, each of whom had lost his right eye. They went disguised as begging friars.

5. **Al Sirat:** the bridge swinging over hell, leading from earth to paradise, according to Mahometan teaching. It was pictured as narrower than a sword's edge, so that those encumbered by a load of sin could scarcely hope to cross it safely.

6. **Aurigation:** the handling of reins.

7. **Pagan Pantheon:** all the gods of Pagan mythology together.

8. **The wrong side of the road:** in England the rule of the road is that vehicles should keep to the left — the reverse of the procedure in America.

9. **Quartering:** a technical word, meaning to avoid a rut or obstacle.

10. **A shilling a day:** the pay of a soldier in the regular army.

RALPH WALDO EMERSON (Page 103)

RALPH WALDO EMERSON (1803–82) was born in Boston and educated at Harvard College, where he graduated in 1821. Five years of teaching were followed by a period of theological study, and a brief pastorate in the Second Unitarian Church in Boston. In 1833, frankly avowing his doubts as to some matters of Christian doctrine, he resigned his ministry, and, after a trip abroad, became a lecturer and writer, presenting a highly idealistic philosophy of his own. All his books, including the two volumes of *Essays* published in 1841 and 1844 and his poetry, are full of spiritual significance. Most of his later life was spent in his home at Concord, where he died April 27, 1882.

Emerson's *Essays* resemble Bacon's in being "wisdom" literature, packed with sententious sayings and animated by a shrewd philosophy. Even Emerson's mysticism, which occasionally led him into obscurity, was modified by his New England common sense, and he frequently clarified his ideas with a homely simile. Structurally Emerson's essays, like Bacon's again, suffer from a lack of continuity of thought; they seem often to be made up of interesting but disconnected observations on assigned topics. Autobiographical passages are comparatively rare, and the author has no intention of revealing his inner self, as did Montaigne and Hazlitt.

Compensation (page 102)

This selection is the third in the volume of Emerson's *Essays* published in 1841. No book in American literature is more stimulating and inspiring than this collection. All the essays are of the highest order; but *Compensation* has been chosen for use here because, while it is somewhat simpler and clearer than the others, it is also completely illustrative, not only of some of the author's most important ideas, but also of his methods as a writer.

1. Emerson was in the habit of placing before each essay a motto of his own in verse, much as a preacher begins by quoting a text.

2. This is a reference to the following essay on *Spiritual Laws*.

3. **Res nolunt, etc.**: Emerson's translation is given in the preceding sentence.

4. The Greek quotation — translated by Emerson in the following sentence — is from a lost play of Sophocles.

5. **Thasians**: inhabitants of the island of Thasus in the Ægean Sea.

6. **Phidias**: the greatest of Greek sculptors.

7. **Polycrates**: the tyrant of Samos, who, considering himself too fortunate, threw his valuable emerald ring into the sea, only to have it returned to him in the stomach of a fish. Shortly after he was betrayed by his own subjects and crucified by his enemy, the satrap of Sardis. Herodotus, the Greek historian, tells the story.

8. **Leger**: an obsolete form of "ledger."

ROBERT LOUIS STEVENSON (Page 128)

ROBERT LOUIS STEVENSON (1850–94) was born in Edinburgh and began his career as a writer in 1876. Despite the fact that he was constantly fighting sickness, he managed to produce no small amount of work. Following a long trip to California in 1879 he married an American lady, Mrs. Osbourne. In 1887, he came again to the United States and settled at Saranac Lake, hoping to benefit his tuberculosis; in the spring of 1888, however, he began a series of cruising trips in the South Seas, and finally took up a permanent residence in Samoa. There he died suddenly, December 3, 1894.

Stevenson's position in nineteenth-century English literature is secure. With remarkable versatility he attempted successfully several branches of literature, including novels, poems, plays, short stories, essays, and letters. Nearly everything he wrote is fresh, attractive, and stimulating; it is expressed, moreover, in a style which is graceful and animated. As an essayist he treated many subjects in delightful fashion. His romantic temperament, his exuberant personality, his eager curiosity, and his facile manner of writing are all singularly fascinating. It was his part to revive the Familiar Essay once made famous by Lamb and Hazlitt.

Crabbed Age and Youth (page 128)

This essay is included in *Virginibus Puerisque* (1881), which contained work already published in various magazines. It is, of course, a vindication of young manhood, couched in a tone of exaggeration in order to emphasize the point.

1. **Clarissa,** one of the earliest of English novels, was written by Samuel Richardson (1689–1761) in 1748. The story is told entirely in letters.

2. **Icarus,** who had been fitted by his father, Daedalus, with wings fastened on with wax, rashly flew too near the sun. The wax melted, and the boy fell into the sea.

3. **The charge at Balaclava:** the famous charge of the Light Brigade made by the English, October 26, 1854, against the Russians, during the Crimean War. Tennyson's well-known poem commemorates the heroic incident.

4. **William Harrison Ainsworth** (1805–82), the author of many mediocre novels.

5. "If youth but knew, if age were only able."

6. **Hernani:** an early romantic drama by Victor Hugo (1802–85), which, in 1830, aroused great enthusiasm in Paris.

7. **Calvin:** the great Swiss theologian (1509–64).

8. **John Knox** was a Scotch religious reformer (1505–72).

ARTHUR CHRISTOPHER BENSON (Page 144)

Mr. Arthur Christopher Benson, the well-known living poet and essayist, is the son of a former Archbishop of Canterbury. Mr. Benson, who is one of three brothers, all distinguished in literary fields, was born April 24, 1862, and received his education at Eton and at King's College, Cambridge. For some years he was a Master at Eton, where he commenced his career as an author. Recently he retired from that position in order to become a Fellow of Magdalene College, Cambridge, where he now resides.

Mr. Benson is a facile writer, and more than a score of volumes already stand to his credit. Chief among them are several collections of charming essays, including *The Upton Letters* (1905), *From a College Window* (1906), *Beside Still Waters* (1907), *At Large* (1908), and *The Silent Isle* (1910), and others no less important. Mr. Benson treats many subjects, and always with suggestiveness and interest. His style is smooth and harmonious, combining some of the characteristics of Walter Pater with some of those of Stevenson. He is always urbane, unruffled, and fluent. His point of view is that of the cultivated scholar and polished gentleman, and accordingly his appeal is mainly to persons with a background of culture.

Books (page 144)

Books is taken from the volume entitled *From a College Window*. The collegiate atmosphere so noticeable in much of Mr. Benson's work is evident here from the very start. The perfect clearness and admirable structure of this essay make it a model for students to follow. It is worth observing how the author proceeds from the material to the idealistic elements of his subject, even concluding with a kind of discussion of life itself. The last few paragraphs are fine examples of a rich and eloquent prose style, passionless, it is true, but still decidedly impressive.

SAMUEL McCHORD CROTHERS (Page 158)

MR. SAMUEL McCHORD CROTHERS is probably the best-known of contemporary American essayists. Born in Oswego, Illinois, on June 7, 1857, he studied for the ministry, and has been, since 1894, pastor of the First Unitarian Church in Cambridge, Massachusetts. He has been for some years a regular contributor to the *Atlantic Monthly*, and his essays have been collected in several volumes, including *The Gentle Reader, Among Friends*, and others.

As an essayist Mr. Crothers belongs to the same literary family as Oliver Wendell Holmes. His work is genial and witty, often whimsical and paradoxical. His style is allusive, abounding in apt metaphors and illuminating, if unexpected, turns of expression. More, perhaps, than any living writer he has succeeded in reproducing the manner of the classic masters of the Familiar Essay; but he has done this, not through imitation, but through a method entirely his own.

The Evolution of the Gentleman (page 158)

The essay is reprinted from the volume entitled *The Gentle Reader*, published October, 1903.

1. **Wat Tyler:** an English peasant who raised an insurrection in 1381, and was slain by William Walworth, Mayor of London.
2. **Plutarch:** a Greek philosopher and moralist (A.D. 46?–120?), who wrote the lives of many famous Greeks and Romans.
3. **Morte Darthur:** a prose romance published in 1485 by William Caxton and written by Sir Thomas Malory.
4. **Night Thoughts:** a gloomy philosophical poem published in 1742–44 by Edward Young (1681–1765).
5. **Course of Time:** an exceedingly dull poem in blank verse written in 1727 by Robert Pollok.
6. **Benvenuto Cellini:** a Florentine artist (1500–71), who wrote a fascinating *Autobiography*.
7. **Beau Nash:** a notorious fop and dandy of the eighteenth century.
8. **Lord Chesterfield:** a statesman and writer (1694–1773) distinguished principally for his fine manners. His *Letters* were sent to his natural son, Philip Stanhope.
9. **Roger de Coverley:** the old Tory knight in Addison and Steele's *Spectator*.

AGNES REPPLIER (Page 176)

Miss Agnes Repplier, the well-known lecturer and essayist, was born in 1857 in Philadelphia and educated at the Sacred Heart Convent, Torresdale, Pennsylvania. Since 1885 she has devoted her attention mainly to literary work, contributing to magazines, especially to the *Atlantic Monthly*, and publishing at intervals volumes of collected essays. Among her best books are *Books and Men* (1888), *Points of View* (1891), *Essays in Idleness* (1893), *Compromises* (1904), and *Americans and Others* (1912).

Miss Repplier's most conspicuous characteristic is a delightful and delicate vein of humor, which underlies all her work. Her essays are generally of a literary type, either about books or authors, or else with a bookish flavor, due to many references to writers and their productions. Her style is remarkably even,

The titles of her essays are usually well chosen, being often in the form of paradoxes or epigrams.

The Mission of Humour (page 176)

The Mission of Humour is taken from *Americans and Others,* Miss Repplier's latest volume. The subject is a difficult one, but it has been a favorite with essayists; Hazlitt and Mr. Crothers, among others, have written delightfully on humor. This particular essay illustrates Miss Repplier's gentle and subtle irony, her trenchant satire, and her apt method of bringing quotations and allusions to bear on her topic. A work of such recent date should be sufficiently clear without annotation.

LE BARON RUSSELL BRIGGS (Page 192)

LE BARON RUSSELL BRIGGS was born in Salem, Massachusetts, April 1, 1857, and was educated at Harvard University, to which place he returned as Instructor in English. Since 1902 he has been Dean of the Faculty of Arts and Sciences at Harvard. Dean Briggs, who has written and lectured frequently on school and college problems, exerts a wide influence among educators to-day, and is recognized as speaking with wisdom and authority on matters connected with university life.

The Transition from School to College (page 192)

This essay, reprinted from *School, College, and Character* (1901) is included here because it illustrates the usefulness of the Essay as a means of talking informally to young men. It must be added also that Dean Briggs's work has a real literary value, apart from the sane advice which it contains.